"He is

9. 33: 3

Right
On Time!

Right On Time!

By

Dr. John N. Hamblin

SWORD of the LORD PUBLISHERS

Post Office Box 1099 • Murfreesboro, Tennessee 37133

All Scripture quotations are from
the King James Bible.

Printed and Bound in the United States of America

This bound volume of sermons is affectionately dedicated to my precious mother, Mrs. Madeline Hamblin. It was the sixteenth president of the United States, Abraham Lincoln, who said, "All that I ever hope to be, I owe to my angel mother." Certainly this preacher would have to say "amen!" to that tribute. For well over a quarter of a century, she has supported her son's ministry from her knees, purse and, above all, her heart. Thank you, Mom, for always being in our corner!

Contents

Foreword

Why another book of sermons? Well, the Bible gives us the answer to that question: "It pleased God by the foolishness of preaching to save them that believe." (I Cor. 1:21). God uses the preaching of the Word to save the souls of men who will believe. The Book of Romans asks the question: "And how shall they hear without a preacher?"(10:14). The truth is, we need more books of sermons, just like this one!

This book of sermons is from the mind and heart of a preacher. This preacher is called of God, empowered by God and blessed by God as one of the great preachers of our day. Every message is well thought out, well structured and full of content that will stir the heart of the sinner and revive the heart of the saint.

America doesn't need what the politicians are calling for—America needs revival! Dr. John Hamblin's messages will stir the hearts of God's people to revival.

As a full-time evangelist, revival is the longing of

his heart. Week after week, Dr. Hamblin is in a different church and sees the need. Furthermore, day after day he is in the Word of God and therefore knows how that need is going to be met. In these sermons, you will read about the great *need* for revival, but you will also read, from the heart of a man who walks with God and knows the Word, *how* revival will come in your heart.

If you read these sermons with the same heart and intensity in which they were delivered, you will find your heart longing for revival. As our hearts are revived, we will see great numbers of people coming to the Lord. Soul winning is one of the greatest by-products of revival: thus, another book of sermons is needed.

God has His hand on Dr. Hamblin. I have had him preach for me several times and always found the message clear, powerful, biblical and Christ-exalting. I wholeheartedly endorse these messages and would encourage every believer, every pastor and every unsaved person to read them carefully.

May God bless you as you read these great messages from God's man, Dr. John Hamblin.

DR. NORRIS BELCHER
Church of the Open Door
Westminster, Maryland

Preface

I count it a great privilege having been asked to write the preface for this, the second power-packed book of scriptural, spirit-filled and soul-stirring messages by my close, personal friend Dr. John N. Hamblin, whom I both consider and call my older brother in the ministry.

I have known Dr. Hamblin for over twenty years now, and I can say with certainty that neither his preaching nor his pulpit presence has changed. If anything, he is more intense, more influential and, most of all, more in touch with what the church and the individual Christian need than he has ever been before.

Dr. Hamblin is a prince among preachers, a pulpiteer who has literally crisscrossed this country countless times in an effort to bring this nation back to God. I am an eyewitness of his ministry, having been honored to share the platform and pulpit with this man of God on many occasions both here and in other countries. I say this with much purpose, because the messages that you are about to read have blessed me personally, and I have seen God use them time and time again to see souls saved, lives changed and genuine revival come to God's people.

There is no doubt in my mind that the evident hand of God rests upon the life and ministry of this seasoned veteran of the faith. This being said, it is with great joy and blessing that I am able to recommend this, another great work from the preacher's pen— "Right on Time" by Dr. John N. Hamblin.

DR. LAWRENCE MENDEZ
Open Door Baptist Church
Detroit, Michigan

1
God Is Always on Time!

"Blessed is he that considereth the poor: the LORD will deliver him in time of trouble.

"The LORD will preserve him, and keep him alive; and he shall be blessed upon the earth: and thou wilt not deliver him unto the will of his enemies.

"The LORD will strengthen him upon the bed of languishing: thou wilt make all his bed in his sickness.

"I said, LORD, be merciful unto me: heal my soul; for I have sinned against thee.

"Mine enemies speak evil of me, When shall he die, and his name perish?

"And if he come to see me, he speaketh vanity: his heart gathereth iniquity to itself; when he goeth abroad, he telleth it.

"All that hate me whisper together against me: against me do they devise my hurt.

"An evil disease, say they, cleaveth fast unto him: and now that he lieth he shall rise up no more.

"Yea, mine own familiar friend, in whom I trusted, which did eat of my bread, hath lifted up his heel against me.

"But thou, O LORD, be merciful unto me, and raise me up, that I may requite them."—Ps. 41:1–10.

1

If you will just hang in there when you encounter problems and troubles, you will experience the next three verses.

> *"By this I know that thou favourest me, because mine enemy doth not triumph over me.*
>
> *"And as for me, thou upholdest me in mine integrity, and settest me before thy face for ever.*
>
> *"Blessed be the Lord God of Israel from everlasting, and to everlasting. Amen, and Amen."*—Vss. 11–13.

His Person, His Power, His Punctuality

The punctuality of a powerful God is one of the greatest truths that could ever reach a person's heart.

Human history, stories from the Scriptures and testimonies from thousands all echo this same truth. Christians can eliminate a great deal of stress and sorrow and many sleepless nights from their lives if they will simply remember that He who is the great and powerful God of the universe and the God of the ages is always punctual. God, who *is* God, is a right-on-time God—never tardy, never a no-show, never forgetful, never failing and never off schedule.

There are two significant words in verse 1: "deliver" and "time." The word "deliver" here means to save and to do it speedily; "time" means from sunrise to sunset.

The testimony of Psalm 41 is that God was always on time in David's life. God has never been late, and He will never be early. He will always be exactly, precisely, right on time.

I. God Is Right on Time When Feeding His Children

"And the ravens brought him bread and flesh in the morning, and bread and flesh in the evening; and he drank of the brook."—I Kings 17:6.

While the prophet Elijah was by the brook Cherith, every morning and every evening he was fed by the ravens. There was a devastating drought in the land, and the Lord sent a band of hungry, carnivorous birds to deliver food to an obedient preacher! Talk about "carry-out"! If that wasn't amazing enough, God had placed that preacher right beside a babbling brook.

Oh, I can hear Brother Elijah saying, "You can keep your Happy Meal. I'll take my heavenly meal!"

In another Psalm, David tells us, "I have been young, and now am old; yet have I not seen the righteous forsaken, nor his seed begging bread" (Ps. 37:25).

Any believer who has spiritual gray hair should be the first to stand up and say, "There have been many times when God has put sustenance in my stomach, provisions in my pantry and refreshments in my refrigerator."

How wonderful is the punctuality of God in providing for His children!

God has been good to us. He has provided us with breakfast in the morning, lunch in the afternoon and dinner in the evening. In fact, God often provides a snack in-between! He is always on time when feeding His children.

Several years ago I was holding a revival meeting at

3

the Community Baptist Church in Garden City, Michigan. It was a special blessing for me because it was nearby and I could preach every night and be at home every day.

One day while my wife was preparing lunch, the phone rang. I answered it and heard the voice of one of our dear deacons, and he told me that he wanted to bring us some fresh vegetables. As soon as I told my wife, she began to weep. She said, "As I was preparing lunch, I was thinking about having a fresh tomato." That deacon brought us several fresh tomatoes with the other vegetables, but that wasn't the end of God's provision.

A man in our church has a very large farm, and after I preached that night, he handed me a big brown bag of tomatoes...but God still wasn't done.

The phone was ringing when I got home. I put down my bag of tomatoes and answered the phone. It was my dear mother, and she said, "John, today someone brought me some vegetables. I can use everything but the tomatoes; they are yours if you want them."

God not only provided for us, He provided in abundance!

God is always on time when it comes to bringing in the groceries and feeding his children, whether it's tomatoes or steak.

II. God is Right on Time When Financing His Children

"Notwithstanding, lest we should offend them, go thou to the sea, and cast an hook, and take up the fish that first cometh up; and when thou hast opened his mouth, thou shalt find a piece of money: that take, and give unto them for me and thee."—Matt. 17:27.

Jesus and the disciples needed money to pay their taxes. He didn't say, "Organize a stewardship campaign," or, "Start a building program." He very quietly and simply gave Peter a five-word solution: "Go thou to the sea."

The Lord said, "Go fishing, Peter. You will catch a fish with a coin in its mouth. Use that coin to pay our taxes."

This miracle mirrors the omniscience of Christ in two marvelous ways. One, He knew which fish in the sea had a coin in its mouth. Two, He knew that it would be the first fish that Peter would catch.

Isn't that just like Jesus! This miracle didn't just occur to Him; He knew all about what was needed, and He was right on time with the solution.

Malachi, chapter 3, gives us a wonderful promise that God will be right on time in helping to finance His children—*if* they tithe. It says that if a man does not tithe, he is a robber; therefore, if you are a God-robber, He may not be right on time. If you have God's tithe in your pocket, you are stealing from Him, and you cannot claim this promise that He will provide for you.

If you are in college, you may be thinking, Tithe or school bill; school bill or tithe? The answer is: Always tithe! If you will tithe, God will provide the financial wherewithal to take care of the school bill. You cannot justify being in Bible college if you are robbing God of His tithe. But, oh, when we tithe, God will be right on time in financing His children.

There are several avenues on which God travels in order to put funds into the hands of a tithing, needy believer. I will give you three of them.

1. God uses people. "For even in Thessalonica ye sent once and again unto my necessity" (Phil. 4:16). Individuals, both unsaved and saved, have been moved by Heaven to open their wallets to the child of God.

2. God uses prayer. "If ye shall ask any thing in my name, I will do it" (John 14:14). You can pray for money. Christians can, through supplication, ask God for certain dollar amounts, but only *if* they can attach the holy, blameless name of Jesus to it.

3. God uses providence. "[He] made his own people to go forth like sheep, and guided them in the wilderness like a flock" (Ps. 78:52). Many times the answer finds its way to the Christian when there is no explanation except God certainly did it! How wonderful when God breaks through, when something happens that you can attribute only to God!

The president of a seminary was facing a financial need in connection with his school. He interrupted one class that was being taught by the great Harry A. Ironside, and he asked him to pray for this need. It is reported that Mr. Ironside stopped teaching and immediately prayed, "Lord, the world is Thine and the cattle upon a thousand hills. Sell a few and send the money here, we ask in Jesus' name, amen."

Before the class period ended, a registered letter came to the seminary president. It read, "I've never met you, but I've heard of your school. I own a lot of cattle, and the Lord has led me to sell a few and send along the money. Enclosed is a check for $10,000."

The check met the school's need to the very penny!

By the way, sometimes people think that a preacher has no special needs, especially if he wears cufflinks and drives a nice car. But preachers do have needs. We do not live on Easy Street; we live on Daily Bread Street. We do not have money trees growing on our property, nor do we live high on the hog, although I do like pork chops.

There are many people who would come to our aid if we shared our needs, but, as a child of God, we go to our Heavenly Father and share the need with Him. So don't think that your pastor has no needs, just because he is not wearing a frown or he is wearing cuff links.

III. God Is Right on Time When Freeing His Children

*"And suddenly there was a great earthquake, so that the foundations of the prison were shaken: and immediately all the doors were opened, and every one's bands were loosed."—*Acts. 16:26.

Luke the physician tells us that when Paul and Silas were in prison, a supernatural earthquake took place and shook the foundation and opened their manacles. As a result, these two preachers were released from prison.

Isaiah 42 tells us, "I the LORD...will...open the blind

eyes, to bring out the prisoners from the prison, and them that sit in darkness out of the prison house" (vss. 6, 7).

No matter the bondage or the danger, even in the jailhouse, God is still able to work with His supernatural power.

There is no reason for any Christian to be in bondage. No matter what you face, what you are going through or what you are up against, you can have liberty, and you can have freedom.

If any people in the entire world should have freedom, it should be those who are saved. If any people in the entire world should be a liberated people, it should be those who know the Lord. Still, there are many, many Christians who struggle under great bondage, but it is not God's fault that they are in bondage. God saved us to be free, and we can go to Him and get that relief, that freedom, that we need from whatever the bondage happens to be.

Sometimes the smallest problem, the minutest incident, will have a Christian all consumed in the bondage of fear and confusion. God is not the author of either; therefore, they are bound up in sin. That sin of bondage will waste the Christian's money and destroy his health, and his testimony will become absolutely worthless.

You don't have to be in bondage. God wants to give you liberty; He wants to give you freedom; He wants to give you relief.

A few years back I was in a revival meeting in Massachusetts. One afternoon the phone rang in my motel room. It was the pastor, and he was down at the front desk. He said, "Dr. Hamblin, I'm here with another man from my church, and I want to bring him to you. He has something that he needs to talk to you about. Will you help him?"

I told him that would be fine, and in a few minutes they were standing at my door. We sat at a little table, and this man began to share his problem.

He had been addicted to a certain thing that was keeping him from being used of the Lord. (I won't tell you what was keeping him in bondage, because maybe you might think your sin is less sinful and hold on to it.)

He said, "I want relief. I want freedom. I want to get this thing off my back. I want God to use me, but I know He can't with this thing in my life."

He sounded genuine about finding relief, so I took him to the Word of God. He got down on his knees, and we began to pray: "God, I want to get up a different man. God, I want to get up with freedom. God, I want to get up with this thing off of my heart so I can be used of You."

I wish you could have seen his countenance when he got up. His face showed that the burden was erased from his heart. He left that motel room a different man than when he came in.

Later in that same meeting, he came to me and said, "The bondage is gone!"

No matter what it is that has you all tied up and burdened down, if you'll but mean business with God, He will mean business with you, and He will bring about your freedom.

I heard about a man named Mr. Johnson who was serving as a chaplain in the South Pacific during World War II. He went on a bombing raid on an enemy-occupied island several hundred miles away.

The mission was a complete success, but on the homeward course, the plane began to lose altitude, and the engines faded out. A safe landing was made on a strange island. The enemy was just one-half mile in each direction, yet the landing had gone undetected.

The staff sergeant came to the chaplain and said, "You've been telling us for months about the need for prayer and a belief that God answers prayer in time of trouble and that He does it right away. Well, we're out of gas. The base is several hundred miles away, and we're surrounded by the enemy."

The chaplain immediately began to pray and take hold of God's promises. He believed that God would work a miracle.

About two o'clock in the morning the sergeant awakened and felt compelled to walk to the water's edge. There he discovered a metal float that had drifted up onto the beach. On the float was a gas barrel. In a few hours the crew reached their home base safely.

An investigation revealed that the skipper of a U.S. tanker, finding his ship in enemy-infested waters, had his gasoline cargo removed so as to minimize the danger in case of a torpedo hit. The barrels were placed on metal barges and put adrift six hundred miles from where the chaplain's plane was forced down.

God had used the wind and the current to navigate

one of those barges six hundred miles and then beach it fifty steps from the stranded men.

Don't forget, Christian, the Heavenly Father will go to great lengths in coming to the rescue of His children. He can and He will free His children.

The Bible shows us that God is always on time, no matter the situation or the need. He has been on time in the past, He is on time in the present, and He will be on time in the future.

This is a truth that can hang a spiritual sun in the Christian's darkest night: God is never one minute early or one minute late: *He is always on time.*

2
In the Fullness of Time a Saviour Came

"Thy throne, O God, is for ever and ever: the sceptre of thy kingdom is a right sceptre.

"Thou lovest righteousness, and hatest wickedness: therefore God, thy God, hath anointed thee with the oil of gladness above thy fellows.

"All thy garments smell of myrrh, and aloes, and cassia, out of the ivory palaces, whereby they have made thee glad.

"Kings' daughters were among thy honourable women: upon thy right hand did stand the queen in gold of Ophir."—Ps. 45:6–9.

Most people, both in and out of the church, have never come to the conclusion that the Lord Jesus Christ left the bliss of Heaven to come to the blight of earth. His birth in Bethlehem was the door He used to enter this world, and His ascension outside Jerusalem was the door He used to exit this world. By the way, He left His exit door open for us to follow. During the Lord Jesus Christ's earthly ministry, He was on an eternal mission.

Psalm 45 is a messianic psalm—or song—that pictures the Lord Jesus Christ as the royal Bridegroom. This chapter can be considered under the following topics:

His beauty—vss. 1, 2
His battles—vss. 3–5
His bounties—vss. 6–9
His bride—vss. 10–17

As the psalm is dealing with God's bounties, it gives a heart-moving phrase about the Person of the Lord Jesus Christ: "All thy garments smell of myrrh, and aloes, and cassia, out of the ivory palaces, whereby they have made thee glad." You see, Jesus is not just a Person who appears on the pages of the New Testament; He is the second member of the Trinity who appears on the pages of the Old Testament as well.

T. DeWitt Talmage, that great and powerful preacher of yesteryear, once wrote about our text: "Some of the palaces of olden time were adorned with ivory. Ahab and Solomon had their homes furnished with it." He pointed out that these palaces are types of Heaven and then said, "What a place Heaven must be!...Not so many castles on either side of the Rhine as on both sides of the river of God—the ivory palaces!"

Why did Jesus come "out of the ivory palaces"?

I. To Fulfill the Scriptures

"Think not that I am come to destroy the law, or the prophets: I am not come to destroy, but to fulfil.

"For verily I say unto you, Till heaven and earth pass, one jot or one tittle shall in no wise pass from the law, till all be fulfilled."—Matt. 5:17, 18.

14

In this Scripture, the Lord Jesus Christ told His disciples that the purpose of His coming to earth was to fulfill the promises of Scripture.

The term "the law, or the prophets" has to do with the first five books of Moses and the rest of the Old Testament. "One jot or one tittle" has to do with the smallest Hebrew letter in the Hebrew alphabet and the small mark of that letter that serves to distinguish one letter from another, like the bottom stroke of the capital *E* distinguishes it from a capital *F*. The Son of God believed in a literal inspiration of the Bible, even in what others thought were small and unimportant details.

John 15:25 says, "But this cometh to pass, that the word might be fulfilled that is written in their law, They hated me without a cause." Mark it down—every message Jesus preached, every miracle He performed, every move He perpetuated was a powerful culmination of a prophecy that pertained to Him.

We can come to Sunday school and the preaching service and come back on every night of the week for the revival services, carrying the King James Bible and knowing that it is the voice of God all because Jesus came.

Some time ago, two friends—one a general and the other a colonel—were on a train talking about their Civil War days; both men were infidels. Their conversation eventually turned to the Person of the Lord Jesus Christ in religion.

They thought it a shame that this historical Jesus had become so incrusted with supernatural superstition. They continued debunking various gospel miracles as legends and myths. Finally the general suggested, "Someone ought to write a book about the real Jesus." The colonel agreed and then said, "General, you should do it. You should portray Jesus as He really was—a mere man and nothing more!"

He began to research the life of Christ carefully, intending to *prove* that He was only a man and not divine. His book was finally completed and published. Its subtitle was "A Tale of the Christ." It became a best-seller, and over two million copies have been sold to date. A movie of the book has also proven to be one of the most popular motion pictures of all time. The title of the book and the movie is *Ben Hur.* The general's name was Lew Wallace; the colonel who challenged him was Robert Ingersoll, one of America's great agnostics.

While General Lew Wallace was investigating the Person of Jesus, it dawned upon his soul that Jesus was *not* man but the Son of God, and he became a sincere believer in the divinity of the Lord Jesus Christ.

It is a scriptural impossibility to look with an open mind at the prophecies connected to the Person of the precious Potentate without coming away saying, as the centurion said centuries ago, "Truly this man was the Son of God" (Mark 15:39).

II. To Furnish the Spirit

"Nevertheless I tell you the truth; It is expedient for you that I go away: for if I go not away, the Comforter will not come unto you; but if I depart, I will send him unto you."— John 16:7.

Here the Lord Jesus Christ told His disciples that the Comforter could not come until He (Jesus) had departed this world. The Holy Spirit that was coming would give to the believer an empowerment, encouragement, enlightenment and enthronement.

In the Old Testament, the temple was a building; in the New Testament, the temple is a body. So when you got saved, the Spirit of God moved into your heart and took up permanent occupancy. As a child of God, you never take a step that He does not take with you. You never travel a mile that He does not travel with you. You cannot go anywhere without Him, because when you got saved, He moved in.

I couldn't be a joyous Christian if it wasn't for the Third Person of the Trinity who moved in the moment I met the Master! He walks with me and talks with me and goes everywhere with me! Every day He works in my life and ministers to my soul!

There is never a day that comes or goes that the Spirit of God does not work in the lives of the saved. Look at all the exciting things He does for the believer.

1. He convicts them. "For the flesh lusteth against the Spirit, and the Spirit against the flesh...so that ye cannot do the thngs that ye would." (Galatians 5:17). It is the Holy Spirit who says no to the Christian who is staring at the pleasure park of sin.

I feel sorry for Christians who only know what sin is when it is preached in church. Don't get me wrong; it is the preacher's responsibility to describe, define, detail and denounce sin, but there is a far better Preacher who lives in your heart if you are saved—the

Holy Ghost. He will convict you of bad attitudes and of bad actions.

2. He calls them. "As they [certain prophets and teachers] ministered to the Lord, and fasted, the Holy Ghost said, Separate me Barnabas and Saul for the work whereunto I have called them" (Acts 13:2).

If you are in the ministry today, it should be because one day the Holy Ghost said to your heart, 'Separate yourself for the work whereunto I have called you.' By the way, the ministry is not a career; it is a calling. I believe we would have revival in our fundamental, independent, Bible-believing, Bible preaching, premillennial, missions-minded, soul-winning churches if some preachers got out of the ministry, because God never put them in the ministry.

The ministry is not about what we can get out of it; it is about what we can put into it. It is a God-called ministry, not man-called.

Twenty-five years ago I left darkness and met the "Light of the World"; I was born into the family of God. Two weeks later I was called into the ministry of the Gospel. It wasn't man that called me; it was God that called me.

3. He comforts them. "And I will pray the Father, and he shall give you another Comforter, that he may abide with you for ever" (John 14:16).

It is exciting that the Holy Spirit comforts us every day. It is the Holy Spirit that whispers to the heart of the believer who is at the open grave of a loved one or is in the physician's examining room. It is He who is with us at the close of a burdensome day, saying, "I am with thee."

We can go through anything and everything because the Spirit of God lives within us. He comforts us.

It is a burden to start a church where there isn't a church, and I know a family that is doing just that—and with two sick children. The Holy Spirit of God is living in their bodies, and He will encourage them, strengthen them, help them and give them power to go on.

I don't like going through difficult times, but I do like it when I get through them and get to the other side. Then I can look back and say, "Look what God did!" It's not, "Look at what I did," but what God did!

Sometimes there is more month than money, but God pulls you through. When you face a wall or an obstacle, instead of whining and whimpering, dial down the drama. Some people can't even go to the grocery store without some type of drama. A Christian can face anything because the Spirit of God is within each child of God.

Among those reading this, there is probably a myriad of burdens and broken hearts; but it is comforting to know that if we are saved, the Spirit of God helps every one of us through that time.

I saw this on a church marquee: "God not only brings you to it; God brings you through it." Why don't you let God bring you through it—whatever "it" may be?

If every Christian who is reading this message would only realize the exciting things that the Holy Spirit does for them: He convicts them, He calls them and He comforts them!

19

A missionary working among an African tribe had tried hard to explain to her native helpers the meaning of the Comforter. She explained the ministry of the Holy Spirit as He encourages, exhorts, admonishes, protects and guides the Christian.

They exclaimed, "Oh, if anyone could do all of that for us, we'd say He is the one who falls down beside us."

Let me explain the phrase, "The one who falls down beside us." When porters carrying heavy loads on their heads go on long journeys, they may become sick and straggle to the end of the line of carriers. Finally they may collapse and be killed and eaten by wild animals during the night. If someone passes by and sees them prostrate and stoops to pick them up, they say, "He is the one who falls down beside us."

Christian, aren't you glad that in this land of sin and sorrow there is One who falls down beside you? That One is the Holy Spirit.

III. To Find the Sinner

"For the Son of man is come to seek and to save that which was lost."—Luke 19:10.

The Lord Jesus Christ told His detractors and His disciples that the primary purpose of His coming to earth was to pursue people for their eternal salvation.

We must keep in mind that these words fell from the lips of the Lord as He was having a meal in the home of Zacchaeus, a crooked tax collector before his conversion. The reason the Lord found His way to this fallen planet was so people could be saved.

Charles Haddon Spurgeon, that "prince of preachers," commented, "Sinners are not only so lost that they need saving, but they are so lost that they need seeking as well."

I don't want to be harsh, but sometimes in my meetings either the pastor or the moderator will say, "Does anyone have a testimony?" Someone will stand and say, "I'm so glad that I found God." Wait a minute! *We don't find God,* because He has never been lost! He has never stopped at the filling station of eternity to ask an attendant for directions. We don't find God; *He finds us* because we are lost!

We are so lost that we not only need saving, we need seeking as well.

Why did He come? He came to find sinners. He came to save the lost, to redeem those that need to be redeemed, and that is the world. And He is still in the soul-saving business today!

A number of years ago I was holding a revival meeting in an inner city. During the day people went out from the church and blitzed the area, leaving tracts and fliers inviting people to the tent meeting. A man who lived not too far from the church came home one afternoon after his shift and found a flier and a tract. He became very upset that they had been left for him, and he wadded them up and threw them away.

The church people went out the next day and, forgetting that they had already been on that man's street, again put out tracts and fliers. The man came home and found them, and again he wadded them up and threw them away—again upset. The next day the church people again forgot that they had been on that street, and for the third time they left the man a tract and a flier. This time when the man came home, he called up his daughter and said, "I'm going to go to that church that is having that tent meeting and give them a piece of my mind!"

He didn't have a Bible, so he borrowed his daughter's King James Bible and went to the tent meeting. He said to an usher, "I want to meet with the pastor! I've got something to say to him!" (Now remember, there is no accident with Providence.) The usher said he didn't know where the pastor was but that he would find him and tell him that this man wanted to see him.

The usher found the pastor and said, "There's a man here who is mad, and he wants to talk to you."

So the pastor came to me and said, "There's a man here who is mad, and he wants to talk to *both of us!* What do you think we should do?"

I said, "Stay away from him now and talk to him after the service. Let's see what God will do."

That night we had singing and the preacher preached; then there was more singing, after which I preached. I gave the invitation, and that man who had been so mad when he came to church literally ran down the aisle, shaking like a leaf in a storm, saying, "Somebody get me to God! I'm lost!" That night he looked into an open Bible and was born into the family of God.

He got baptized during that meeting; he joined the church during that meeting; he met a wonderful woman, and they got married; he's now a deacon, and he sits on the front row of the church. Once a month he calls me and leaves a message on my voice mail, and it always starts the same way: "Dr. Hamblin, I don't know where you're preaching in America tonight, but thank God that you preached the night that I got saved! And keep preaching, because there are others out there like me that need what I've got now."

I was at a meeting in Maryland, and construction work had blocked the road in front of the church. We had great crowds, but I'm sure the construction work hindered some. As we left the service on Thursday night, a woman holding a bright light and wearing a bright orange vest was directing all traffic to the left. I felt impressed to turn right, and she came running over to my car. Before she could say anything, I said, "Wait a minute, ma'am. I'm not going to run the blockade. You're probably going to be here all night, and I just want to give you something to read. It's from the Bible." She thanked me and I left.

On Friday night as we were leaving the church, I saw her standing out there directing traffic to the left. I turned right, and this time before I could say anything she said, "I've been looking for you. I read that little green book that you wrote, I prayed that prayer on the back, and I asked the Lord to save me. On the other end of the street are my friends, and last night I gave them your little book and asked them to read it and pray the prayer."

Christian, if Jesus came to save the sinner, we ought also to be looking for them.

After reading Psalm 45:8, Henry Barraclough was

inspired to write the beautiful hymn, "Ivory Palaces." The chorus says:

> Out of the ivory palaces
> Into a world of woe—
> Only His great eternal love
> Made my Saviour go.

Jesus came "out of the ivory palaces" to fulfill the Scriptures, to furnish the Spirit and to find and save the sinner!

Jesus is looking for you if you're lost. It is not an accident that you are reading this, because there are no accidents with Providence. God wants to save you. Through His love and mercy and grace He has brought you this material, and the Spirit of God is moving upon your heart right now. What you need to do is to say yes to Jesus!

I pray that the Lord will do a deep and lasting work in each Christian's heart. May the spark of revival be ignited in our souls, and may that spark turn into an everlasting flame.

3
Take Time to Smell God's Roses

"And David rose up early in the morning, and left the sheep with a keeper, and took, and went, as Jesse had commanded him; and he came to the trench, as the host was going forth to the fight, and shouted for the battle.

"For Israel and the Philistines had put the battle in array, army against army.

"And David left his carriage in the hand of the keeper of the carriage, and ran into the army, and came and saluted his brethren.

"And as he talked with them, behold, there came up the champion, the Philistine of Gath, Goliath by name, out of the armies of the Philistines, and spake according to the same words: and David heard them.

"And all the men of Israel, when they saw the man, fled from him, and were sore afraid.

"And the men of Israel said, Have ye seen this man that is come up? surely to defy Israel is he come up: and it shall be, that the man who killeth him, the king will enrich him with great riches, and will give him his daughter, and make his father's house free in Israel.

"And David spake to the men that stood by him, saying, What shall be done to the man that killeth this Philistine,

> and taketh away the reproach from Israel? for who is this uncircumcised Philistine, that he should defy the armies of the living God?

> "And the people answered him after this manner, saying, So shall it be done to the man that killeth him."—I Sam. 17:20–27.

There are three words in verse 26 that you should underline, if not in your Bible, then certainly in your mind. The words are "the living God"!

One of the most powerful truths that could ever penetrate Christian hearts would have to be the truth that God is alive. The moment that this becomes real to believers, prayer, the Christian life and soul winning will become much more meaningful to them. It is impossible to meditate upon this truth without being transformed by it.

In chapter 17, we read of David's defeat of Goliath. The story is one of the most familiar narratives in the Old Testament. The entire chapter contains the following sections:

> The opportunity—vss. 1–23
> The obstacles—vss. 24–30
> The overwhelming victories—vss. 31–58

While conversing with some of the soldiers of Israel about the giant Goliath, David says, "For who is this uncircumcised Philistine, that he should defy the armies of the living God?"

The word "living" just means that He is alive. The phrase "the living God" is used in the Bible thirty times.

David knew something that every child of God needs to know: God is alive! You say, "Preacher, that is ridiculous. Christians know that." Oh, yes, they know it mentally, but do they know it spiritually? They know it in their heads, but do they know it in their hearts? How well do we realize that He *is* the living God?

There are several reasons why I know God is alive.

I. He Changes Sinful Lives

I know God is alive because He changes sinful lives.

> *"And Zacchæus stood, and said unto the Lord; Behold, Lord, the half of my goods I give to the poor; and if I have taken any thing from any man by false accusation, I restore him fourfold."*—Luke 19:8.

One day the Lord Jesus Christ visited the city of Jericho. A dishonest tax collector named Zacchaeus was so desirous to see Him that he climbed up into a sycamore tree to get a good view. When Jesus passed by the tree, He looked up, called him by name and asked him to come down out of the tree.

I'm not sure of the exact spot, but somewhere between the top and bottom branches of the tree, Mister Zacchaeus became Brother Zacchaeus and was born into the family of God!

The first thing Zacchaeus did after his salvation experience was to tell the Lord Jesus Christ that he was going to give half his goods to the poor and make fourfold restitution for all the money he had gained dishonestly.

I believe that God is alive because He changes sinful lives. D. L. Moody once said, "When a man begins to make restitution, it is a pretty good sign of conversion."

Isaiah 59:1 says, "Behold, the LORD's hand is not

shortened, that it cannot save; neither his ear heavy, that it cannot hear."

I'm glad that God is still in the business of changing sinful lives. If that were not true, this pulpit would be empty tonight; if that were not true, these seats would be empty tonight; but, hallelujah, God is still in the business of changing sinful lives.

There are three tools that God effectively uses to change the unbeliever. Anytime an unbeliever has been changed—I'm talking about regeneration, not reformation—God has used one, two or all three of these tools.

1. The Holy Scriptures. "Being born again, not of corruptible seed, but of incorruptible, by the word of God, which liveth and abideth for ever"(I Pet. 1:23).

It may be a preached sermon, it may be a gospel tract, it may be a quoted verse, but behind every conversion experience is the Bible.

This afternoon when I went to lunch, in the short time I was there, I passed out some gospel tracts. You know, God can take just one gospel tract that was handed out at a fast-food restaurant and use it in a marvelous way.

2. The Soul Winner. "And he [Andrew] brought him [Peter, his brother] to Jesus"(John 1:42).

The Infinite has chosen the finite to play an important part in preparing people for eternity. God will never use you in a greater way than as a soul winner.

3. The Holy Spirit. "And when he [the Holy Spirit] is come, he will reprove the world of sin, and of righteousness, and of judgment"(John 16:8).

The Holy Spirit is the Third Person of the Trinity who works behind the scenes when someone is saved.

Whenever anyone believes and trusts Jesus as his Saviour, it is the Holy Spirit who is working behind the scenes.

Oh, that every person reading this would realize the effective tools that God uses in changing the unbeliever.

It is easy to hide a sin from man, but it is *impossible* to hide a sin from God! You might be able to pull the wool over man's eyes, but you can never fool God.

I have a dear friend who, at one time in his life, had a serious drug problem that was unknown to his family and friends. We have been friends for more than twenty years; we grew up together, went to church together and couldn't be any closer if we were biological brothers.

He was taking mind-and-body-destroying chemicals, until late one night when he wrote a desperate note to God. It said: "God, I need help!" He folded that note and put it in a green Bible and deliberately pushed it under his bed. In a few short weeks, God answered that note by saving his soul. That man is now a pastor of a fundamental church and a professor in a fundamental Bible college.

I know God is alive because he changes sinful lives.

II. He Answers Serious Prayers

I know God is alive because He answers serious prayers.

"And when he had considered the thing, he came to the house of Mary the mother of John, whose surname was Mark; where many were gathered together praying."— Acts 12:12.

One day the apostle Peter was placed in a prison and headed for certain martyrdom. Believers in the early church gathered at Mary's home for an emergency prayer meeting. They weren't having a cookie party or a candle party or a cosmetics party. It was a prayer meeting where they bombarded the throne of grace with their heartfelt petitions.

Because of that prayer meeting, God sent an angel on a heavenly errand. That angel went down to the prison and freed the preacher, and before the prayer meeting was over, the one they were praying for arrived. What an answer to prayer!

My friends, we need to realize that God is alive and He answers serious prayers.

Often we read the Bible too rapidly, and we don't let the words penetrate our hearts. You may be able to read *War and Peace* rapidly, but you ought not to read the Word of God rapidly! You need to *pause* at every comma, *stop* at every period and realize that this is the written voice of God, because the Bible is how God speaks to us.

Some time ago I was reading Acts, chapter 12, and I wrote down seven different miracles that Peter witnessed in that jail escape.

1. Peter escaped from four quaternions of soldiers who were guarding him. "Quaternion" was the name given to a company of four of Herod's army. That means sixteen men were guarding Peter.

2. Peter was freed from the chains that connected him to the soldiers.

3. Peter was guided by a light that illuminated the prison but did not startle the guards or the prisoners that were sleeping.

4. Peter heard the angel speak, but no one else heard a single word that the heavenly messenger spoke.

5. Peter had heavy chains fall from his hands, but no one heard them hit the cell floor. If I were to ask you to be silent and then took a songbook and dropped it, you would hear it even on this padded platform. But the cell floor was not padded, and yet no one heard a single sound.

6. Peter walked through two different wards without being noticed.

7. Peter did not even touch the huge iron gate, and yet it opened.

Friend, I believe that God is alive because He answers serious prayers. Psalm 50:15 says, "Call upon me in the day of trouble: I will deliver thee, and thou shalt glorify me."

There are many with burdens and broken hearts in every prayer meeting. I don't know what you are going through or what you are facing this hour, but I do know this: There is a God in Heaven who answers serious prayer. There is a God in Heaven whose ears are bent toward the prayers of His children.

I know that He is there, and I know that He is alive, because He answers serious prayers.

There was a small party of missionaries who had

gone to Tibet to minister to the people. At first the missionaries were hated. One night the Tibetans encircled their houses, holding flaming torches. They began dancing around in a wide circle which kept diminishing in size as they got closer to the houses, intending to set them ablaze.

The wild chanting came closer and closer to the houses, and the missionaries fell to their knees in prayer. They prayed so intently that they never realized when the chanting stopped. When they arose, the mob had dispersed, and they were allowed to remain.

Years later, one of the Tibetan converts told the missionaries that he was in that mob before he was saved. He said that they had every intention of burning the missionaries to death in their homes; however, as they approached the dwellings, there stood before the door a figure in white apparel holding a flaming sword. They fled in fright, and thus the door was opened for the Gospel in Tibet!

God answers serious prayers.

III. He Gives Sizable Victories

I know God is alive because He gives sizable victories. I deliberately used the word "sizable" because it means "BIG."

> *"The children of Israel walked upon dry land in the midst of the sea; and the waters were a wall unto them on their right hand, and on their left."*—Exod. 14:29.

One day the prophet Moses stood on the shore of the Red Sea with the nation of Israel. It was not very long until they heard the fast-approaching chariots of Pharaoh.

Picture it in your mind. Moses is standing before the deep Red Sea. The discouraged children of Israel are beside him, and behind him was the destroying Egyptian army.

Do you know what I think disturbed Moses the most? It wasn't the deep Red Sea; it wasn't the destroying army of Egypt; it was the discouraged people of God!

Discouragement is contagious. If you get around a Christian who is living in the valley of discouragement and depression instead of living on the mountaintop of victory, it won't be long until you are dragging your lip too.

I look at some Christians who seem to be everlastingly dragging their lips on the ground, walking around like God's dead children. The worse thing you can do is to ask them, "How are you today?" They will tell you the truth, and when they're done you need a six-week revival meeting to get you back up.

But Moses, the man of God, had the answer. He lifted his rod over the sea, and the sea divided. God's chosen people crossed over without a single one of them getting his sandals wet or muddy.

Then Moses again lifted his rod over the sea, and the Egyptian soldiers that were hot on their heels were covered by water.

I believe God is alive because He gives sizable victories.

"For the LORD your God is he that goeth with you, to fight for you against your enemies, to save you."—Deut. 20:4.

Isn't it only reasonable to believe that if God can give a nation a mighty triumph over a deep sea and a destroying army, He can give any one of His children a mighty triumph over anything that he comes up against? Isn't that reasonable?

He gives sizable victories, and that's the reason you ought to know that He is alive!

One of the most famous legions in the Roman army was the Thundering Legion. The Thundering Legion was the name given to the military legion in the days of the philosopher-emperor, one of the worst persecutors of the church, Marcus Aurelius (A.D. 121–180). Tertullian tells how the legion won the name "Thundering Legion."

In A.D. 176, the army of the emperor was engaged in a campaign against the Germans. In their march, the Romans found themselves encircled by high mountains which were occupied by their savage enemies. In addition to this danger, the army was tormented by thirst because of the drought.

It was then that the commander of another legion-informed the emperor that this particular military legion was made up of Christians and that they believed in the power of prayer.

"Let them pray, then," said the emperor.

Soldiers of the legion then bowed on the ground and earnestly besought God in the name of Christ to deliver the Roman army. They had scarcely risen from their knees when a great thunderstorm arose, accompanied by heavy hail.

Storms drove the barbarians out of their stronghold, and, descending from the mountains, they entreated the Romans for mercy. His army delivered from death at the hands of the barbarians and from death by the drought, the emperor decreed that this legion should be thereafter called the "Thundering Legion." It also abated somewhat his persecution of Christians.

O Christian, the same God who gave victory to the Thundering Legion, the same God who gave victory to the children of Israel, can give us victories—sizable victories!

I know God is alive because He changes sinful lives, He answers serious prayers and He gives sizable victories.

Moses had to do something in order for the sea to divide. It was Moses' faith that helped him lift that rod over the Red Sea. You too have to believe God for victory in your personal life, your family life or whatever area or realm where you need victory. God will give sizable victories.

4
It's Time to Head Back Home

"And he arose, and came to his father. But when he was yet a great way off, his father saw him, and had compassion, and ran, and fell on his neck, and kissed him.

"And the son said unto him, Father, I have sinned against heaven, and in thy sight, and am no more worthy to be called thy son.

"But the father said to his servants, Bring forth the best robe, and put it on him; and put a ring on his hand, and shoes on his feet:

"And bring hither the fatted calf, and kill it; and let us eat, and be merry:

"For this my son was dead, and is alive again; he was lost, and is found. And they began to be merry."—Luke 15:20–24.

Every believer, no matter how long he has been saved, knows of at least one person who is a prodigal. It may be a son or daughter, a brother or sister, a parent or someone with whom you used to share a church pew. When these straying individuals eventually turn their hearts for home, they should be able to see some exciting things on the horizon as they do so.

In Luke, chapter 15, you find three stories given by Jesus. They concern:

The lost sheep—vss. 1–7
The lost shekel—vss. 8–10
The lost son—vss. 11–32

In verse 20 there is this wonderful text: "And he arose." Have you ever considered what the Prodigal found when he finally turned his feet toward his father's farm? It is absolutely amazing when you think of it.

John R. Rice penned this about this powerful phrase: "I once pictured in my mind the long road home, the deep concern, the tired steps. Would the father receive him and forgive him, or would the father scorn him? But as I meditated further, I noted that it was not a long way home. That boy might have been a thousand miles from home, but as far as this parable is concerned, it was only a step. If one in deepest sin turns heart and face toward God, He is there!"

It is important for the wayward believer, the prodigal, to return to the will of God; but it is also imperative for us to remember that when he does come home, he is entitled to the full privilege and benefits of the Father's house.

Those in the Father's house must make sure that there are some exciting things already set up for those who are this moment starting back from a far country. It is my conviction that even as we consider the matter, there *are* prodigals packing up and heading home. I am burdened for these prodigals, but it is also my burden that those who have been faithful have things in place for the ones who are coming back.

When the Prodigal shook himself loose from the clutches of the far country, he started an arduous journey retracing his steps back home to his father's house. He was shocked when he arrived home. Having totally blown it, he was unprepared for what he found there.

I. The Prodigal Found a Waiting Father

"And he arose, and came to his father. But when he was yet a great way off, his father saw him, and had compassion, and ran, and fell on his neck, and kissed him."—Vs. 20.

The father with his hopeful eye on the distant horizon spotted the wayward, weary son long before he ever reached the property line. The Word of God is strangely silent on how long the patient parent remained looking for his straying son. We do know that the moving of the clock hands and the turning of the calendar pages did not affect the longing of the father's heart. He was truly a longing father; consequently, he was a looking father. His longing and his looking never faded, because in the depths of his heart he was also a loving father. Longing, looking and loving when he saw his son "a great way off," he became a long-distance running father.

T. DeWitt Talmage once wrote about this stirring scene: "He ran—no wonder! He didn't know but what the young man would change his mind and go back; he didn't know but what he would drop down from exhaustion; he didn't know but what something fatal might overtake him before he got to the doorsill, and so the father ran."

Friend, those of us who have stayed faithful in a father's house must make sure that there is a father waiting for those that are starting back from a far country.

The Bible says, "Charity [that's love in action] suffereth long, and is kind; charity envieth not; charity vaunteth not itself, is not puffed up" (I Cor. 13:4). Mark it down: no wayward believer is ever going to head toward home if he senses that nobody there will be eager to welcome him back.

I have observed wayward children of God who finally came back to the house of God but found not one child of God who made an attempt to throw out the welcome mat.

It doesn't matter that the backslider comes back looking, acting and smelling like the world. The "father...had compassion," a spirit strangely missing so often. He ran, fell on his son's neck and kissed him. Before the Prodigal had a chance to get the scent of the hogpen off him, he already had been draped with the silk of the home place.

When people come back to church, they need to be welcomed. It doesn't matter if they look rough or bad; take it easy with them. Chill out! Don't be so uptight! The church is a spiritual hospital, a spiritual first-aid station, and we ought to thank God when people come to the house of God. Compassion will welcome them and love them. We should be glad that they're here instead of in a bar or some other Devil's den in the back alley. They need to come to the house of God. There they will get the answer they need from the Word of God! A warm welcome from God's people will go a long way. Many a prodigal has started back but not stayed back because nobody welcomed them back.

When prodigals come back to the church, it is not the duty of the members to begin correcting and scolding them. The stench and the scars of the pigsty will be obvious, but there is a right way to go about dealing with the problem. The spiritual hospital, the church, is to give hope, help and healing. So don't blow them out of the water until there is time for God to work on them and minister to them. Don't forget, at one time you or someone in your family was exactly the same way!

God help you if you hinder somebody who is trying to come back to the Lord. They need a steppingstone in front of them, not a stumbling block. They are not singing in the choir—not yet! They are not a teacher or a deacon—not yet! So be patient and pray for them.

In a seaport in Maine a young woman promised her sailor-fiancé that she would keep a light burning in her window every night until he returned. He sailed the next day, and his vessel was never heard from again, yet his fiancée kept the light burning until her death fifty years later.

For five full decades, 18,262 times, she lit that lamp as a message to her fiancé that said, "I'm waiting for you, and I believe you are coming back."

If a woman whose heart went down with her fiancé's ship could watch and wait for him for five long decades, why can't we who are saved keep a light of love and longing burning for our brothers and sisters who are still in a far country?

Every church ought to have a light burning in the window that will say, "The light is on in this church, and we're waiting for you to come back."

The first time I preached this message, when I got to the point where I said, "The prodigals are coming! The prodigals are coming! It could be that they're on the property right now, that they're already at the front door," the church secretary jumped up in the middle of the service and ran out. I later learned that she ran into the foyer and looked for her wayward boy, then out to the parking lot to see if he was there.

Three months passed, and she came to hear me preach in another meeting. There she said to me, "You were right! My prodigal boy has come back! He has gotten right with God! You were so right! The prodigals were coming. They do come home!"

They're still coming to their senses while mired deep in the stench of the world's pigsty. They're still leaving the far country and making that lonesome trek toward the father's house. When they get there, there ought to be a waiting father.

II. The Prodigal Received a Warm Forgiveness

"And the son said unto him, Father, I have sinned against heaven, and in thy sight, and am no more worthy to be called thy son.

"But the father said to his servants, Bring forth the best robe, and put it on him; and put a ring on his hand, and shoes on his feet."—Luke 15: 21, 22.

While the son was humbly repenting, the father

was hastily reprieving and requesting some heart-moving items.

This is the very same attitude that obviously dwelled in the heart of Abraham Lincoln when someone asked him, "What will you do when the South is defeated and when the Union is restored?"

He answered, "I will treat them as if they had never been away."

Those of us who are saved in the Father's house must be sure that there is a warm forgiveness readily available for those who come back from the far country.

If there is little or no forgiveness in your Christianity, then you are not practicing Bible Christianity. You may not be lost, but if there are grudges and bitterness that hold sway in your life, you are certainly backslidden. You may not be the prodigal that needs to come back from the far country, but you are a prodigal all the same.

The father gave his backslidden son a warm forgiveness. His example sets the standard for us and for our ministry. That standard ought already to be in place in the church before the prodigals get back.

The Bible is a divine Book of precise detail. Everything that is in the Bible is supposed to be there. It is the inspired, inerrant, infallible and impeccable Word of God. If you are weak on the Bible, then you will be weak on everything else. When you are weak on the written Voice of God, you've got spaghetti for a backbone.

The waiting father's open arms of welcome say volumes about the warmth of his forgiveness.

43

1. The Royal Robe. "Bring forth the best robe, and put it on him."

The best robe was only worn by special people on special occasions, and this garment speaks of the covering from the nakedness and nastiness of the world.

2. The Regent's Ring. "Put a ring on his hand."

This circular piece of jewelry was a mark of identification as well as authority.

Note that the Prodigal did not put on the robe or the ring. The father said, 'Put the robe on him. Put the ring on him.' He told the servants to put them on his son, because the son would not have put them on himself. He had said, "I have sinned against heaven, and in thy sight, and am no more worthy to be called thy son."

When people get right with God, we need to help put the robe and the ring on them. You never know when you may need that.

When prodigals get away from the Lord, they're not excited about singing in the choir or opening the service with prayer or even reading their Bible in their own home.

I want a ministry that puts robes and rings on people, a ministry that will encourage and bless and strengthen and inspire and motivate. It's easy to be a hindrance, but I want to be a helper.

The best of us is no better than the worst of us. I read a sign that said, "If you were to kick the person who gives you the most trouble, you'd not be able to sit down for a month!"

3. The Regal Shoes. "Put...shoes on his feet."

There is a distinction between the shoes in Bible times and the sandals of Bible times; and the father gave his son shoes, not sandals.

I was preaching this message in a revival, and a college student was outlining the message. Under shoes he had written "the Reeboks." That was a good guess, but they were not Reeboks; they were *regal* shoes.

Our churches ought to be known as places where people can come and get right with God, where if you blow it and absolutely mess up, you can get right with God and get back on your feet. And that is putting on the robes, the rings and the regal shoes.

I saw a sign on a church marquee the other day that said, "If you're not perfect, this is the church for you." That is the way the house of God ought to be—helping people, strengthening people and giving them what they need so they can go on in the Christian life. If we don't do it, pray tell, who will? If we don't do it, pray tell, who will help us when we need help?

The robe, the ring, the regal shoes—here we have a complete covering; thus, the truth is communicated by the thought that forgiveness is final, covering is complete, salvation is successful.

Oh, that every Christian would realize the thrilling items that pass from the Father's hand to a found son's heart and say volumes about forgiveness—the robe, the ring and the regal shoes.

Did you know that the rebel can become the repentant? The backslider can come back! The wayward can return!

A young man in his teens occupied a compartment on a railroad train with only one fellow passenger, an older man who was an evangelist. They had not spoken, but as the young man was looking worried, the preacher sympathetically asked if something was wrong, thus winning the lad's confidence.

The youth opened his heart to the older man and told him that he'd run away from home and disgraced his family and brought shame to their name. Now the repentant young man wanted to return home.

He said, "I wrote Mother, and she wants to receive me, but Father said no. She said she was going to try and talk him into accepting me. She reminded me that the train I'd have to ride to come back home runs through the family property. 'But,' she said, 'there's a garden out by the tracks, and next to it there is a tree. If I've convinced Father, I will hang a white cloth on the tree.'"

The evangelist said, "Son, don't be concerned; I'll look for you."

After several miles the boy spoke again: "We're getting close to my home. Look for that one, lone, white rag hanging from the tree next to the garden."

As the train whizzed past the property, the evangelist turned to the boy and said, "The tree is *covered* with white rags."

There ought to be a tree somewhere on every church's property covered with white rags, so as prodigals come back, they'll know there is a pardon before they ever get there.

46

III. The Prodigal Received a Wonderful Festival

"And bring hither the fatted calf, and kill it; and let us eat, and be merry:

"For this my son was dead, and is alive again; he was lost, and is found. And they began to be merry."—Vss. 23, 24.

Before the son even finished speaking, the father ordered steaks and arranged a celebration.

In a revival meeting I made mention that everybody in Luke, chapter 15, was happy about the return of the Prodigal Son with the exception of the elder brother. A woman came to me after the service and told me there was someone else who wasn't happy about the younger son's return—the fatted calf!

See the younger son making his way home. With every climb of the hill, with every crossing of the stream, he is rehearsing his speech that will bring about his reception at home.

I think Charles Haddon Spurgeon would have been impressed to hear his speech; William Shakespeare and Winston Churchill would have been envious of his words—but he didn't get a chance to give his speech. The reason is that there was no need for it; his father's actions spoke much louder than the son's words would have.

When the backslidden prodigals come back, they're back. They don't need to make a speech or give reasons why they left or came back, and no one should ask them why! There is no need for a press conference when the prodigals return.

47

"Merry" is used twice in these verses; it means "to be jolly, to indulge in hilarity, to feast with mirth." If you put your ear to the Word of God, you can still hear the inspired wind carrying back the noise of that celebration as the father and hired servants "began to be merry."

> Ring the bells of Heaven; there is joy today
> For a soul returning from the wild!
> See, the Father meets him out upon the way,
> Welcoming His weary, wand'ring child!
>
> Glory! Glory! How the angels sing;
> Glory! Glory! How the loud harps ring!
> 'Tis the ransomed army, like a mighty sea,
> Pealing forth the anthem of the free.
> —William O. Cushing

Those of us abiding in the Father's house must be sure we have a wonderful festival already set up for those who are coming back from a far country.

The Bible says, "Is any merry? let him sing psalms" (Jas. 5:13).

What is the right response of a spiritual Christian in a scriptural church when a sorrowful Christian returns? It should be horns, hats, confetti and a large number of people shouting, "Let's party! The prodigal is back!"

Some time ago I was having a meal with a preacher after a revival service. Because of some problems, this dear preacher had been out of the ministry for a period of time. He went to a church that provided a place of hospitality and recuperation for him. He asked me if I would come preach for him when he got his spiritual sea legs back. I immediately said yes.

Shortly thereafter he took a church, and I went to preach a revival meeting for him. He told me later that after he'd gotten right with God, on a Christmas morning he had called a preacher in another state. It was a man that he thought was his friend. He was told, "Get your family all together, move to a distant state, go to a church where nobody knows you—but don't think about joining. Sit on the back row and don't do anything. After ten years, call me, and maybe you'll be able to do a little something for the Lord." That response is *nowhere* in the Word of God.

This preacher sat there weeping because he thought his so-called friend would encourage him and give him good counsel. I reached across the table and wrote three words on the paper placemat and signed my name. I handed it to him and said, "I'm glad you're back in the saddle. More importantly, God is glad that you're back in the saddle. The next time you see that preacher who gave you that bad counsel years ago, give him this placemat."

The three words were: "That is stupid!"

I praise God that He is still forgiving and receiving prodigals!

If God is happy, it does not matter who else is unhappy. If God is smiling, it does not matter who is frowning. If God is in your corner, it doesn't matter who is in the other corner.

Theodore Roosevelt said, "In my opinion, the story of the Prodigal Son is the most beautiful story in all of the English language."

It might be that more prodigals would come back if

they could only hear from the Father's house our rejoicing over the last prodigal that returned.

My burden is not just for those that are out in the far country, but it is for those Christians in the Father's house. The crowd who stayed home needs to have the house in order—love, compassion, forgiveness, reconciliation, restitution—everything in place when the prodigals turn their feet toward home.

Let's get it ready!

They're coming! They're coming!

The prodigals, wasted and weary, are coming!

The prodigals, bowed, bent and broken, are coming!

The prodigals, derelict, dirty, diseased and down, are coming!

They're coming! They're coming! They're coming!

5
In the Time of Storm

A few years ago someone gave my name to a reporter who was writing an article on "The Preaching of Fundamentalists." That's what I am, and I make no apology for it. This reporter called me, and in the course of the interview, he asked me, "What kind of sermons do fundamentalists preach?"

I thought about that for a moment and then said, "Basically, there are three types of sermons that a fundamentalist preaches. First, there are salvation sermons; second, there are strengthening sermons; and third, there are soul-winning sermons."

In a salvation sermon, we are preaching to see sinners saved *in* the service; but in a soul-winning sermon, we are preaching to encourage the saved to go after the unsaved so the unsaved might be saved *outside* the service. With that said, my goal here is to give you the second type of sermon—a strengthening sermon.

From time to time the people of God need messages

of strength and of solace. Some would have us believe that every time a preacher stands to preach he needs to skin people. But if you skin anything, it's either dead or it's going to die. While I do believe in shearing the sheep awfully close sometimes, I don't believe in skinning people when I preach. So with the help of the Lord, I want to give you what I hope will be a strengthening sermon.

> "And straightway he constrained his disciples to get into the ship, and to go to the other side before unto Bethsaida, while he sent away the people.
>
> "And when he had sent them away, he departed into a mountain to pray.
>
> "And when even was come, the ship was in the midst of the sea, and he alone on the land.
>
> "And he saw them toiling in rowing; for the wind was contrary unto them: and about the fourth watch of the night he cometh unto them, walking upon the sea, and would have passed by them.
>
> "But when they saw him walking upon the sea, they supposed it had been a spirit, and cried out:
>
> "For they all saw him, and were troubled. And immediately he talked with them, and saith unto them, Be of good cheer: it is I; be not afraid.
>
> "And he went up unto them into the ship; and the wind ceased: and they were sore amazed in themselves beyond measure, and wondered."—Mark 6:45–51.

Please look back at verse 48: "And he saw them toiling in rowing; for the wind was contrary unto them: and about the fourth watch of the night he cometh unto them, walking upon the sea, and would have passed by them."

I want to focus my thoughts on the seven-word phrase "for the wind was contrary unto them," as we consider the subject "In the Time of Storm."

Most Christians fail to understand that the cyclone is often the best and most blessed classroom. Truths learned in a tempest are usually remembered for a lifetime. When God chooses to send a saint through a spiritual hurricane, it is never so he will suffer hurt but always so he will receive substantial help.

The time of storms! In our text we find the Lord Jesus Christ walking upon the Sea of Galilee. Surely this miracle proves that Jesus is the Son of God. Peter could not walk upon water by his own power. Contrary to what they may tell you, no politician can walk on water. Only the Son of God, God the Son, could ever perform this miracle of walking upon the Sea of Galilee.

This story is one of seven divisions in this chapter:

A story of unpardonable foolishness—vss. 1–6
A story of unusual things—vss. 7–13
A story of unrestrained fear—vss. 14–29
A story of unique fellowship—vss. 30–32
A story of unlimited feeding—vss. 33–45
A story of unfailing friendship—vss. 46–52
A story of unexpected fame—vss. 53–56

In this inspired story of unfailing friendship, we see a person called to take his seat in the lecture hall of hard winds and high waves. "The wind was contrary unto them." The word "contrary" means "clashing or conflicting." A parallel verse to Mark 6:48 is John 6:18, which says, "And the sea arose by reason of a great wind that blew." A great Bible student of another century wrote, "Storms may often rise against us even when we are acting in direct obedience to the will of Christ."

Never forget that if the followers of the Lord were enrolled in the University of Tempests yesterday, then the followers of the Lord will be enlisted in the same University of Tempests today. If you miss everything else in this chapter, I pray that you will not miss that.

Friend, you and I, those of us that are saved, will at some time in our Christian lives sit in the classroom of storms. I can only imagine that out of all those reading this there are those who are in a tempest, a cyclone, a storm; and I come to you with the good news that you *can* make it, you *can* handle it, you *can* get through it.

Let us notice three colossal truths that the believer should learn from the schoolhouse of heavy storms. They are all found here in Mark, chapter 6.

I. The Classification

"And straightway he constrained his disciples to get into the ship, and to go to the other side before unto Bethsaida."—Mark 6:45.

A colossal truth that the believer should learn from the schoolhouse of heavy storms has to do with the classification of the storm. In this verse we learn that at the bidding of the Lord Jesus Christ His entire close band of followers got into a boat to journey across the Sea of Galilee to Bethsaida. We must take note of two important words that bump into each other in this interesting narrative: "his disciples."

You do not find one word in the Old Testament and

54

the other word in the New Testament. You do not find the first word in one chapter and the other word in another chapter. You do not even find one word in one verse and the other word in another verse. Here they are right next to each other—"his disciples." These intriguing words mean "belonging to a male individual" and "those who uphold a party."

Here is a golden nugget of truth from the gold mine of the Bible. The omniscient, all-knowing Christ directed those faithful followers who had short haircuts, three-buttoned suits, cuff links, handkerchief in the pocket, pocketfuls of gospel tracts, a Soul-Winner's New Testament in their hands and who had all just come from the midweek prayer meeting into a ship that was destined for a storm. You see, Jesus knew what was going to happen before it ever happened, and it was by the bidding of the Lord Jesus Christ that they entered this ship that was headed for a storm.

Now, mind you, Jesus did not have the privilege of the Weather Channel. But the One who controls the weather does not need the Weather Channel. Jesus knew what was going to happen before it ever took place. Here He got the best of the best, the cream of the crop, the A-Team, if you will, and He told them to get into a boat. He sent them across the Sea of Galilee to Bethsaida, knowing that a storm was ready to break.

May I say to you that these were not heathens, not pagans, not sinners, not prodigals, not even wayward Christians. Again Jesus put the best of the best into a ship and sent them into a storm. And may I remind you that a couple of years ago God took one of the best of the best and put him in a storm. God took a great church and put them in a storm.

It was not because of sin; it was because God decided it was good for Dr. George Riddell III and for the Open Bible Baptist Church to take her undershepherd and put him in the hospital. You might not know this, but he was really at the door of death. God thought that was good. God has a way of taking the cream of the crop and putting them in a boat and sending them into a storm.

Here is a news flash that some of us need: Jesus did not tell the carnal crowd to get into the vessel; He told the close Christians to get into the vessel and go to Bethsaida. That's why we had better be careful when we say to someone, "Well, I believe it's the chastisement of God on your life."

When I was a little boy and my mother chastened me, I didn't need any of my little friends to tell me why my mother was chastening me. When she would absolutely beat me within inches of my life, I did not need anybody to come along and say, "By the way, your mother is dealing with you about" whatever it was that I had done. No, I knew she was chastening me and why.

But there are folks that think they are on the Holy Ghost Council; they think it's their job to tell those who are suffering that it is God's chastisement. You had better be careful what you say to another Christian, because it may not be chastisement at all. It may be that they are on the A-Team and God has put them in a boat and sent them into a storm because of how close they are to Him.

Friend, you and I should learn to classify the hard

storms. The Bible says in I Peter 4:12, "Beloved, think it not strange concerning the fiery trial which is to try you, as though some strange thing happened unto you." This fact makes it very clear to the child of God that he is not the only one to have a flat tire, an empty ice tray in the freezer (Why is it always empty when I need ice?), a cell phone drop a call, a goldfish die in a fish bowl, a shirt come back from the dry cleaner missing a button, a letter get lost in the mail, a motel clerk give someone else his reserved room, an order of French fries end up missing when you are going through the drive-through at McDonald's after already driving ten miles down a highway, a policeman issue an unfair ticket (Every ticket I've ever seen has been unfair.), a large unexpected bill, a blanket fall off the bed on a cold winter night, a sincere motive be misjudged, an attempt at character assassination, a so-called friend become a sworn enemy all because of jealousy, a son or a daughter become wayward, a close bosom buddy contract a terminal disease or a precious family member suddenly pass away. Listen, friend, it just could be that you are among the best of the best, the close Christian.

During World War I, a disastrous fire broke out in the Greek city of Salonika. The historic church of Saint Dimitrios suffered considerably from the fire. The scorching heat destroyed the plaster covering of the west wall and exposed a seventh-century painting of Saint Dimitrios fighting a raging fire in his own day. One of the things that the flames through which we pass do is to break through the surface of the years and reveal the souls of saints and heroes of old who fought similar fires, or, one could say, who went through similar storms in their own day.

I encourage you in the school of storms to learn this paramount truth: properly classify the storms.

II. The Observation

> *"And he saw them toiling in rowing; for the wind was contrary unto them: and about the fourth watch of the night he cometh unto them, walking upon the sea, and would have passed by them."*—Mark 6:48.

A second colossal truth that a believer should learn from the schoolhouse of heavy storms has to do with the observation *through* the storm. The word *observation* means "a watch kept on something or someone." This verse tells us that the second the winds picked up and the waves began to pile into the boat, the Lord Jesus Christ perceived it from the top of a mountain peak.

Mark it down—the Saviour always sees His servants and saints when they are in the midst of a serious storm. That encourages me. It absolutely blesses my heart that when you and I are in a storm we are not alone, we are not by ourselves. The pastor may not know about it, the pastor's wife may not know about it, the church may not know about it, but there is One up in Heaven who's keenly aware of it, because He watches us. His eyes are upon us. It's the Lord! He sees us when we are in a storm!

In preparing for this message, I wanted to see if the Bible said anything about where the eyes of the Lord are. Now immediately what comes to your mind, as it did mine, is the verse in the Old Testament that says,

"The eyes of the LORD are in every place, beholding the evil and the good." But I wondered if the Bible was specific. Does the Bible zero in on exactly *where* the eyes of the Lord are this very moment? I discovered that there are places upon which the eyes of the Lord Jesus Christ are fixed this very moment.

This may shock you, but the first place I found Jesus looking was on the Christian's *giving*. Luke 21:2: "And he saw also a certain poor widow casting in thither two mites." It doesn't matter if a child of God puts two cents or two thousand dollars in the offering plate, Jesus sees it. Now if that were the only place He was looking, that would mean that there are some people whom Jesus never sees in church. ("Ouch" is the expression you were searching for!)

By the way, do you like the beautiful decorations in your church? Then thank a tither! Do you like a clean house of God? Then thank a tither! Do you like air conditioning in the summer and heat in the winter? Then thank a tither! Do you like a pastoral staff? Then thank a tither! Do you like speakers coming in and hanging you over Hell and preaching the Devil out of you? Then go ahead and thank a tither!

Where are the eyes of the Lord Jesus Christ right now? They are fixed upon the Christian's giving, but they are also on the Christian's *grieving*. John 11:33 says, "When Jesus therefore saw her weeping, and the Jews also weeping which came with her, he groaned in the spirit, and was troubled." No Christian grapples with grief at the entrance of a loved one's grave without experiencing the compassionate gaze of the Son of God.

Back on January 7, 2007, my mentor, Dr. Tom Malone, Sr., graduated to Glory. No preacher has impacted or influenced my life more than Dr. Malone. The morning of his passing I was there. In fact, on the day before Mrs. Malone had called and asked me to come. As I stood by the side of his bed in St. Joseph's Hospital in Pontiac, Michigan that day, he was coherent. He knew what was going to happen if God didn't over-rule. He knew he was not long for this world. I knew that without a miracle this would probably be the last chance we would have to converse this side of the street of gold, the gates of pearl and the walls of jasper.

I held him in my arms and said, "Dr. Malone, I'll never know why you put such confidence in me. I'll never know why you took me under your wing. I'll never know why you showed such an interest and love and support, but I want you to know by the help and grace of God, I'll never embarrass you. With the help and grace of God, I'll do you proud; I'll not let you down." I leaned over and kissed him twice on the forehead and said, "Good-bye."

Early the next morning the phone call came from Mrs. Malone that Dr. Malone had graduated into Glory.

She said, "Now, John, you know that you are to lead the funeral; you are to speak in the funeral and handle all the funeral arrangements. That's what Dr. Malone wanted."

When the call came, I had a picture on my side of the dresser on the mirror. It was a picture taken of Dr. Malone and me one night in a revival meeting. I remembered the night it had been taken.

I was preaching the meeting, and one night he just showed up. I was out in the lobby, and the service was already underway. The choir was singing, and a young preacher came up to me and said, "You'll never guess who's on the third row waiting to hear you preach."

"Who?"

"Dr. Tom Malone, Sr."

Now I knew that Dr. Malone was not preaching out anymore. I knew that he was not even preaching in town. I knew that basically he was at home and was hardly even going out to get a bite to eat.

I said to that young man, "Right! Sure! Dr. Malone is on the third row. Tell me another one!"

He said, "No, I'm telling you. He's on the third row."

"Is Indiana Jones with him too? Is Elvis sitting next to him? Yeah, sure! Dr. Malone is on the third row."

I walked in, and sure enough, there he sat. I walked up to him and hugged his neck. I said, "What in the world are you doing here?"

"I came to hear you preach!"

"Well, you know how it is with me, Dr. Malone! If you're in the building, I'm sitting and you're preaching."

"I didn't come to hear me preach. I came to hear you."

"Well, I'm not preaching if you are in the building."

"Then if you're not preaching, and I'm not preaching, I guess we'll just stare at each other all night long!"

I got up to preach that night, and I'll never forget that

he had his Bible and followed along. He took out a 3"x5" card and scratched my anemic 2"x4" outline down. When the service was over, the church photographer took a picture of Dr. Malone and me.

Then when the news came of Dr. Malone's passing, I took that picture off my side of the dresser and paper-clipped it to my Bible. Now I carry it with me.

When I preached that morning in a revival meeting, before I went to the pulpit, I glanced at it. All the way up to the funeral, each time I preached, before I took the pulpit, I glanced at that picture. As I led in the funeral and spoke there, and even at the graveside, before I did anything, I took a moment and glanced at it. Still, whenever I go to the pulpit, I glance at it again.

I have to tell you that I miss him a great deal. But I am glad God knows all about that. And I'm glad that one day we will be reunited with those that we love and those who have helped us and those who have encouraged us. I am glad that when you and I grieve that the eyes of the Lord are upon us.

Third, and it may shock you, but the Lord's eyes are on the Christian's *getting away* from God! Luke 22:61 says, "And the Lord turned, and looked upon Peter. And Peter remembered the word of the Lord, how he had said unto him, Before the cock crow, thou shalt deny me thrice." Yes, the eyes of the Lord Jesus Christ are fixed on the Christian who is getting away from God. Just the moment that the backslider realizes that Jesus is looking at him is the minute he starts back toward Jesus. I think this is really a life-changing truth.

Now you are familiar with the story. Peter denied

he knew the Lord, just as Jesus had said that he would. Then the cock crowed, and Peter automatically remembered the words of the Lord. Christians remember the Bible, even when they are backslidden. That's just something that a saved person does.

So Peter backslid and got away from the Lord, and the cock crowed. Then Peter remembered the words of the Lord Jesus. He turned and Jesus just looked at him. I do not think that was a hard look, and I do not believe it was a harsh look. I believe when Jesus looked at Peter, it was a *heartbroken* look. It was a look of pathos, a look of passion. Jesus wasn't happy that Peter was backslidden. Jesus wasn't thrilled that Peter was out of the will of God.

When Jesus looked at Peter, He was broken and He was burdened. If that is the look of Jesus for backsliders, then shouldn't that be the look of the church? That ought to be the look of Christians for backsliders too.

In one revival meeting where I was preaching, a preacher's wayward son came to hear me. I was sitting on the platform and was thrilled when I saw him walk in. I thought, *Man, he's on my prayer list. What an answer to prayer!*

But before I could even get up and preach, before the choir even sang, before they even had the first congregational song, a lady walked up to this preacher's son on the back row, stuck her finger on the edge of his nose and chewed him out. My heart broke because I had prayed for that young man. I had invited that young man. I was hoping when I began preaching and gave him the Scriptures that God would do something to his heart.

Before I could even get up and announce my text, that young man was out the door. To be honest with you, I can't blame him. If Jesus looked at Peter with passion and pathos, then we should look at backsliders the same way. You don't have to condone wrong or compromise with sin—I'm not talking about that. But at the same time, we should have the good sense to have a brokenness and burden for people who are away from God. They are that way because they are out of fellowship with God. They need somebody to love them.

I thought to myself, *That woman's going to answer for what she did.* My Bible still talks about offending one of God's little ones. It doesn't just mean someone small in size. I believe that is someone small in spiritual size. God said it would be better if a millstone was tied around our neck and we were cast into the depths of the sea than for us to offend them (Matt. 18:6). God said that!

The places upon which the Lord Jesus Christ's eyes are fixed include the Christian's giving, the Christian's grieving and the Christian's getting away from God.

A family was enjoying a camping trip. One evening after tucking four-year-old Bobby in bed, they were sitting about the campfire. After a time Bobby called out saying, "I'm not afraid, Mommy! I'm not afraid, Daddy! God is watching over me!"

"You're a big boy," his mother replied. "I know you're not afraid."

However, Bobby soon called out asking his mother to come into the tent.

"I just wanted to tell you *why* I'm not afraid," Bobby said. "You see all those bright stars up in the sky? They are the reason I'm not afraid. You see, Mommy, I know that they must be God's *peepholes.* He can look through them and watch over me."

Aren't you glad that it doesn't matter where you are on the planet or even in the universe? You are under one of God's silver, sparkling peepholes! God is watching you! He is observing you! He knows all about it.

III. The Visitation

Not only do we learn of the classification of the storm and the observation through the storm, but we also learn the colossal truth of the *visitation* in the storm.

> *"And he went up unto them into the ship; and the wind ceased: and they were sore amazed in themselves beyond measure, and wondered."*—Mark 6:51.

The Lord Jesus Christ showed up in the very midst of this storm in which His intimate group of followers found themselves. He stepped into their vessel, and immediately the wind and the waves became still.

For an individual even to come close to appreciating the full weight of verse 51, he must first couple it with verse 48. There the Bible says, "He...would have passed by them."

That six-word phrase is awfully interesting; in fact, it's awesomely interesting! It is a wrinkle in the fabric of this narrative that deserves our attention. Compare it with the account of the disciples walking to Emmaus, where it says, "He made as though he would have gone further" (Luke 24:28), and with the message to the church of Laodicea: "Behold, I stand at the door, and knock" (Rev. 3:20). You will come to the wonderful conclusion that Jesus loves to be *invited* into a troubled ship, a lonely heart or even an indifferent church. What a truth!

Jesus made as if He would pass by. I wonder if I go through some things in my life where Jesus, as He is passing by, wants me to say, "Lord, I need you!" I wonder if there are churches that are going through some storms, some trials, some turbulent times, and Jesus is passing by just waiting to hear someone say, "Help!"

I wonder if there are some homes where people are doing the best that they can to do right and live right and not be a hypocrite, but to be real and genuine and authentic, but it seems like the wheels have come off the thing. It seems like there are more questions than answers. Could it be that Jesus is passing by such a home and is just wanting and wishing and waiting for someone to say, "Lord, help!"

C. A. Tindley must have had this same truth on his heart, for he penned:

> When the storms of life are raging,
>   Stand by me;
> When the storms of life are raging,
>   Stand by me.
> When the world is tossing me
>   Like a ship upon the sea,
> Thou who rulest wind and water,
>   Stand by me.

Friend, you and I should learn from the school-house of hard storms!

6
It's Time to Give It Your All

"Serving the Lord with all humility of mind, and with many tears, and temptations, which befell me by the lying in wait of the Jews."—Acts 20:19.

Most Christians have no idea what they need in their lives to carry out meaningful service for Christ. This explains why the dropout rate is so high among Christian workers. When Christians are made aware of the key elements in service, immediately their labor for the Lord will take on a greater longevity. What does it take to serve the Lord?

Paul's farewell comments in Acts, chapter 20, include a striking phrase in verse 19: "Serving the Lord with all humility of mind."

The word "serving" indicates "to be a slave; to do service; to be in bondage." Whenever we read the Bible and look at the life of Paul, we must remember that he was God's special pattern for the believer: "Howbeit for this cause I obtained mercy, that in me first Jesus Christ might shew forth all longsuffering, for a pattern to them which should hereafter believe on him to life everlasting" (I Tim. 1:16).

We should take a closer look at the things in Paul's life to see what needs to be in our own lives so we can be successful in serving the Lord.

If there is anything I want to be, it is a servant of the Lord. I don't want to be just a saved person or a child of God or a believer—though they are wonderful things. I want to be able to serve the Lord with my heart and my life and my soul.

What a great revival we would have, what a great spiritual awakening we would experience, if the average believer would say, "Yes, I'm saved, and I thank God for it; but I want to be more than saved—I want to be serving the Lord."

There are three things that stand out from the apostle Paul's life that the believer must have to serve the Lord Jesus Christ.

I. Prayer

"And the Lord said unto him, Arise, and go into the street which is called Straight, and enquire in the house of Judas for one called Saul, of Tarsus: for, behold, he prayeth."—Acts 9:11.

It takes prayer for a believer to serve the Lord.

Luke, the physician, tells us that God told Ananias to travel to Straight Street and do a follow-up call on Saul of Tarsus. Ananias was to look for a new convert on his knees. (It is interesting to note that the apostle Paul started and ended his Christian life on his knees.)

We must have prayer in our lives in order to serve

the Lord. The Bible says, "And he spake a parable unto them to this end, that men ought always to pray, and not to faint" (Luke 18:1).

I hardly think about prayer without thinking about an experience in my own life. I was saved in September of 1979, and in November of that same year I was here at Emmanuel Baptist Church and the Midwestern Baptist College for the first time. They used to have Founders' Day the day after Thanksgiving. They had different competitions and preaching contests. The competition was awfully weak that year, and somehow I won. Not only did I get a trophy, but I got to preach in the evening service with Dr. Tom Malone, Sr. What a time—saved in September and preaching with Dr. Malone in November! I learned that day that prayer should be a priority in the life of a child of God.

Mankind today finds itself living in an hour where computers, virtual reality and robotics are effortlessly replacing flesh and blood. But in the eternal work of God, there is no replacement for a kneeling figure.

Have you ever wondered for whom and for what the Christian should pray? The scriptural answer is: for his family (Gen. 17:18); for preachers (Phil. 1:19); for workers (Matt. 9:38); for spiritual blessing (Matt. 6:33); for mercy and grace to help in the time of need (Heb. 4:16); for temporal blessings (Gen. 28:20, 21). Just those few things would be an excellent start for a Christian's prayer list.

It takes prayer to serve the Lord.

I read recently the story of how a friend had asked

Samuel F. B. Morse, inventor of the telegraph, "Professor Morse, when you were making your experiment, did you ever come to a halt, not knowing what to do next?"

He replied, "Oh, yes, more than once."

"And what did you do at such times?"

"I may answer you in confidence, sir, but it is a matter of which the public knows nothing. Whenever I could not see my way clearly, I prayed for more light. I made a valuable application of electricity. Flattering honors came to me from America and Europe on account of the invention that bears my name, but solely because God was pleased to reveal it to me."

Is it any mystery that he officially opened the Baltimore to Washington line by sending in Morse code the message: "What hath God wrought?"

Christian, it would be impossible even to guess at the exciting things God would do in our lives if we would only go to Him in simple supplication like Samuel Morse. Prayer!

II. Passion

"For the love of Christ constraineth us."—II Cor. 5:14.

It takes passion for a believer to serve the Lord. The motivating factor for laboring for the Lord was the meaningful love of Christ. If the Saviour loved the saint enough to *die* for him, then the saint ought to love the Saviour enough to *live* for Him! That ought to be a motivating factor and a meaningful factor in each of our lives.

70

You say, "Is this a passion for the lost, or is it a passion for the Lord?" A Christian who doesn't have a passion for the lost is a Christian who doesn't have a passion for the Lord. A Christian who has a passion for the Lord is a Christian who has an immediate passion for the lost. A Christian needs a passion for the Lord and a passion for the lost—the two are inseparable.

If I'm not the soul winner I ought to be, it's a love problem—I don't love the Lord the way I ought. If I don't have a good word on my lips all the time for Jesus, it's not that I don't love the lost; it's that I don't love the Lord. If I don't have a gospel tract on my person at all times, it's not because I don't love the lost; it's because I don't love the Lord.

When we don't witness, it's not because we don't love the lost; it's because we don't love the Lord. If we love Him and have a passion for Him, then we'll always have a passion for the lost.

I think we're trying to get people to witness who just don't love Jesus. But you will fall fresh in love with the Lamb of God when you think about Him as the One who hung between Heaven and earth for you. Then you'll be a walking, talking witness for Jesus.

Friend, you and I must have passion in our lives to serve the Lord.

There are many reasons why the believer should love the Lord Jesus Christ. I want to give you the three most important.

1. He welcomed us. "And he arose, and came to his father. But when he was yet a great way off, his father saw him, and had compassion, and ran, and fell on his neck, and kissed him" (Luke 15:20).

The first hand you shook when you entered the family of God was a nail-pierced hand.

2. He won us. "Jesus answered and said unto her, If thou knewest the gift of God, and who it is that saith to thee, Give me to drink; thou wouldest have asked of him, and he would have given thee living water" (John 4:10).

Before Jesus saved you, you found it amazing that *One* so wonderful would want *one* so wicked.

3. He washed us. "Unto him that loved us, and washed us from our sins in his own blood" (Rev. 1:5).

He welcomed us, He won us and He washed us. The only right response to a bloody Calvary is a sold-out life!

I may not look like much, but I am washed in a fountain filled with blood, flowing from Emmanuel's veins—"and sinners plunged beneath that flood lose all their guilty stains."

> At the cross, at the cross, where I first saw the light
> And the burden of my heart rolled away,
> It was there by faith I received my sight,
> And now I am happy all the day!
>
> —Ralph E. Hudson

> Jesus paid it all; all to Him I owe.
> Sin had left a crimson stain;
> He washed it white as snow.
>
> —Elvina M. Hall

It is wonderful to be saved. It is glorious to be saved. It is just stupendous to be a saint of God. And it ought to affect us and move us and excite us that we are saved!

You say, "Well, I used to be that way, but I got over it." You got over it? "Well, it's just not my personality to get excited about spiritual things." Do you get excited when your favorite team wins a championship? Do you get excited when you get a raise at work? I'm not against either of those things, but why do you not get excited about being saved?

"I got over it." Unfortunately, that's the truth for too many Christians. If you get excited about temporal things, then how on earth can you not get excited about eternal things?

"But if I got excited, someone would accuse me of having wildfire." I'd rather be accused of having wildfire than to be accused of having *no* fire!

It is exciting to be saved! Oh, if every single believer who is reading this would realize that the reasons why he ought to love the Lord are: He welcomed us, He won us and He washed us!

When Hudson Taylor was examining some young people who had volunteered for the mission field, he wanted to ascertain their qualifications for the arduous life which they were considering.

"Why do you wish to go as a foreign missionary?" he asked one.

"I want to go because Christ has commanded us to 'go ye into all the world, and preach the gospel to every creature,'" (Mark 16:15).

Another said, "I want to go because millions are perishing without Christ, not having even heard of the one name whereby the lost may be saved."

Others gave various answers. After a long period of silence, Mr. Taylor spoke: "All of these motives, howsoever good, will fail you in times of testing and trial and tribulation, possibly death. There is but one motive which will sustain you; namely, 'For the love of Christ constraineth us'" (II Cor. 5:14).

III. Perseverance

"Having therefore obtained help of God, I continue unto this day, witnessing both to small and great, saying none other things than those which the prophets and Moses did say should come."—Acts 26:22.

It takes perseverance for a believer to serve the Lord. Paul stood before King Agrippa and gave him a clear and powerful presentation of the Gospel. It is within this witness that Brother Paul hands the last key to the Christian that unlocks the door to serving the Lord: "I continue unto this day." That phrase is simply perseverance.

Friend, you and I must have perseverance in our lives if we are to serve the Lord: "If thou faint in the day of adversity, thy strength is small" (Prov. 24:10).

It takes perseverance to serve the Lord—the attitude of "I'm not giving up; I'm not turning back; I'm not lying down; I'm not going to blow retreat and raise the white flag of surrender. I'm not going to quit!" In fact, a Christian ought to cut the word "quit" out of his dictionary.

Not everybody is going to be behind you. Not everybody is going to say, "Way to go!" Not everybody is going to be cheering for you or asking you to sign their Bibles. You will find that your biggest fan today can, in less than twenty-four hours, be your biggest foe tomorrow. It takes perseverance.

A young preacher came to me recently and said, "Dr. Hamblin, people are saying things about me."

I said, "Praise the Lord! If they're talking bad about you, then they've stopped talking bad about me!"

Christians think about the silliest things, and they quit over the most infantile things. How can the believer, seeing Paul standing heavily chained before King Agrippa, want to give up because someone didn't speak to him at church, because the pastor didn't visit his home when he had an ingrown toenail, because he didn't see his name in the church bulletin or it was misspelled?

I get excited when my name *isn't* in the church bulletin, because 99.9 percent of the time when it is, they slaughter the spelling. Some of the love-offering checks I receive have "John" misspelled!

Sometimes I'm as happy when some people don't talk to me as when they do. I am finding in my meetings that "Dr." in front of my name means that I am a medical doctor. They will corner me after I preach and show me a scar and ask for my advice on what to do about their health! I certainly don't advise them on medical issues. In fact, I don't advise you to show your scars to me!

If it bothers you because someone doesn't speak to you, spiritually you belong in the nursery.

Some people get upset when the pastor doesn't visit them. Have you ever thought that maybe he was trying to win someone to the Lord? Maybe he's helping some Christian with a *real* problem, and he just can't get to visit you after you've had surgery on your ingrown toenail.

Paul said, "I continue unto this day."

An unknown poet wrote:

> I've taught a class for many years,
> Borne many burdens, toiled through tears;
> But folks don't notice me a bit.
> I'm so discouraged; I'll just quit!
>
> Some time ago I joined the choir
> That many folks I might inspire.
> But folks just don't seem moved a bit,
> And I won't stand it. I'll just quit!
>
> I've led young people day and night
> And sacrificed to lead them right.
> But folks won't help me out a bit,
> And I'm so tired, I think I'll quit!
>
> Christ's cause is hindered everywhere,
> And folks are dying in despair.
> The reason why? Just think a bit:
> The church is filled with folks who quit!

One of our former presidents was defeated in a legislative race when he was twenty-three, failed again in business at age twenty-four, overcame the death of his sweetheart at age twenty-six, had a nervous breakdown at age twenty-seven, failed in an effort to become vice president at age forty-seven and lost a senatorial race at age forty-nine. But he was elected president of the United States at age fifty-one.

If perseverance could carry Abraham Lincoln all the way to the White House, I wonder how far perseverance will carry the child of God.

Thank God that you are in the house of God, but it ought to go a little bit farther than just taking up pew space. It ought to be that you are serving the Lord through prayer and passion and perseverance.

Oh, to have these things in our lives so that we, like Paul, would serve the Lord!

7
Finding Time to Pray

"And he spake a parable unto them to this end, that men ought always to pray, and not to faint;

"Saying, There was in a city a judge, which feared not God, neither regarded man:

"And there was a widow in that city; and she came unto him, saying, Avenge me of mine adversary.

"And he would not for a while: but afterward he said within himself, Though I fear not God, nor regard man;

"Yet because this widow troubleth me, I will avenge her, lest by her continual coming she weary me.

"And the Lord said, Hear what the unjust judge saith.

"And shall not God avenge his own elect, which cry day and night unto him, though he bear long with them?

"I tell you that he will avenge them speedily. Nevertheless when the Son of man cometh, shall he find faith on the earth?"—Luke 18:1–8.

Most Christians struggle with the performance of those paramount things that they should be doing with spiritual pleasure. Even the serious supplicant notes the times when fervency, faithfulness and focus are missing from his secret place. But there are some tremendous truths that will cause the Christian to look at prayer time not just as a duty but truly as a delight.

Our text can be called "the confident prayer," and in it we see the strong command of the Lord Jesus Christ in connection with supplication.

> *"And he spake a parable unto them to this end, that men ought always to pray, and not to faint."*—Vs. 1.

The word "ought" means "to be held or bound in duty or moral obligation."

Dr. John R. Rice said, "It is not only that we should do *well* to pray, but that we *ought* to pray. It is not that we ought to pray *often,* but that we ought *always* to pray."

I want to show you three imperatives given by the Lord Jesus Christ during His earthly ministry when He used the word "ought."

We "ought" to tithe: "Woe unto you, scribes and Pharisees, hypocrites! for ye pay tithe of mint and anise and cummin, and have omitted the weightier matters of the law, judgment, mercy, and faith: these ought ye to have done, and not to leave the other undone" (Matt. 23:23).

We "ought" to pray: "Men ought always to pray, and not to faint" (Luke 18:1).

We "ought" to humble ourselves and minister to others: "If I then, your Lord and Master, have washed your feet; ye also ought to wash one another's feet" (John 13:14).

Jesus did not make a casual suggestion about our praying; He gave us a clear command. It is not something that we do when we can find time; we "ought always to pray."

I want to give you several exciting truths that will encourage each believer to obey the Lord Jesus Christ's command to pray.

I. Prayer Brings the Saviour to Your Tempest

"And he [Jesus] *was in the hinder part of the ship, asleep on a pillow: and they awake him, and say unto him, Master, carest thou not that we perish?"*—Mark 4:38.

The *peril* is the storm; the *prayer* is the sincere word to the Saviour; the *performance* of the miracle is the stopping of the storm.

After a full and fruitful day of preaching, the Lord and His disciples find a ship to ferry them across the Sea of Galilee. A storm comes upon them, and the jostling ship is almost sunk. The disciples cry out, "Master, carest thou not that we perish?"

The Lord arises, then rebukes the wind, the waves and the worrying disciples by saying, "Peace, be still. And the wind ceased, and there was a great calm" (vs. 39).

Amy Carmichael wrote these heart-penetrating words:

Thou art the Lord who slept upon the pillow
    Thou art the Lord who soothed the furious sea.
What matter beating wind and tossing billow,
    If only we are in the boat with Thee?

Every Christian has days of blessing and days of benefit, but we will also face dark skies and distressing seas. During such times we need to recall quickly Psalm 107:29: "He maketh the storm a calm, so that the waves thereof are still."

81

When the winds of adversity and the ways of anxiety beat upon the boat of your life, remember who it is that is with you and how to bring the situation to His attention. Getting Jesus in the ship happened when you got saved, but prayer moves an omnipotent Saviour from the stern to the bow of the saint's storm-tossed ship.

No matter what we go through or are up against, we don't have to get the Lord into our lives because He's already in our hearts. We just need to call the problem to His attention, and He will move from the back to the front!

An old mariner's chart of the East Coast of North America and adjacent waters drawn in 1525 and now in the British Museum had some interesting and fearful directions on it. Across the areas of unexplored land and sea were written the following words: "Here be giants. Here be fiery scorpions. Here be dragons."

That chart fell into the hands of the scientist Sir John Franklin. He scratched out the fearful old markings and wrote: "Here is God!"

When you are in the most terrible tempest, surrounded by giants, fiery scorpions and dragons, "Here is God!" When you talk to Him, He can take charge of the torrent.

Why should the believer pray? Because it brings the Saviour to his tempest.

II. Prayer Brings the Sustenance to Your Table

"Give us this day our daily bread."—Matt. 6:11.

In the Model Prayer the Saviour said that the Christian can request everyday meals. This petition acknowledges our dependence on God for daily food, both spiritual and physical. We are to live daily upon God; therein is our source of supply. We ought to pray because it brings the sustenance to our table.

There are three things that should motivate the believer to pray for "daily bread." Bear in mind, "daily bread" is not just a physical need; it can also be a spiritual need.

1. The powerful revelation of God. "For all the promises of God in him are yea, and in him Amen, unto the glory of God by us" (II Cor. 1:20).

Behind every one of God's promises lies the power to bring to pass the provision of the promise, whether the promise is in the Old Testament or the New Testament.

Some Christians do theological handstands when it comes to some promises: "Well, that's in the Old Testament, so it's not for the dispensation in which I dwell." Not everything in the Bible is written *to* me, but it is all written *for* me.

2. The past record of God. "And the ravens brought him bread and flesh in the morning, and bread and flesh in the evening; and he drank of the brook" (I Kings 17:6).

If God used a brook and a bird to take care of one of His prophets, what makes you think you are going to starve to death?

I've yet to meet a Christian who could be a poster child for world hunger. Shame on any believer who thinks that he will go without!

Dr. Tom Malone, Sr., said that in I Kings, chapter

17, there was a great drought in the land, so those ravens would fly to Ahab's butcher shop and bakery shop and bring the food back to the man of God.

This was the original Meals on Wings, which later became known as Meals on Wheels.

3. The plentiful resources of God. "But my God shall supply all your need according to his riches in glory by Christ Jesus" (Phil. 4:19).

No believer has ever received from the bank of Heaven a notice that he has overdrawn his account.

Remember, the things that should motivate Christians to ask God for "daily bread" are the powerful revelation of God, the past record of God and the plentiful resources of God! Prayer brings sustenance to your table.

Several years ago I was preaching in a tent meeting. I had to contend with hot weather, mosquitoes and one preacher with a bad spirit. But there was a teenage boy there every night. One night as I came in, he threw his arms around my neck, weeping, and said, "Dr. Hamblin, I love you and appreciate your ministry. I don't have any money, but I want to give you a small token of my appreciation." Before I could stop him, he put in my pocket a $20.00 gift certificate to my favorite restaurant. What a thrill for me.

III. Prayer Brings the Holy Spirit to Your Task

"If ye then, being evil, know how to give good gifts unto your children: how much more shall your heavenly Father give the Holy Spirit to them that ask him?"—Luke 11:13.

The gifts that He mentions are the ones that the church and Christians need most.

Charles Haddon Spurgeon said, "If we do not have the Spirit of God, it were better to shut the churches and nail up the doors and put a black cross on them and say, 'God have mercy on us.'"

Someone said that the Spirit of God could move His membership out of the average fundamental, independent, Bible-believing, Bible-preaching, premillennial, mission-minded, soul-winning, temperamental Baptist church, and a month later no one would know that He was not there.

How many times do we just go through the motions of having church? How many times do we meet, but God doesn't meet with us? How many times do we teach Sunday school, preach our services, go out witnessing and endeavor to do the work of God without that enduement that comes from the Holy Spirit.

Psalm 62:11 says, "God hath spoken once; twice have I heard this; that power belongeth unto God."

Prayer is the holy conveyer belt that moves God's power from Heaven to the believer's heart.

The paramount need in the fundamental church is that there be Spirit-filled people in the pulpit, the choir, the Sunday school classroom, the church bus and the youth department.

Every preacher needs God's power, but every layman needs that *same* power. You don't need education or some letters behind your name; if you are a Christian, you need that presence from another Country. You need that anointing that only comes from God's power.

I wept as I read the story of one of Dwight L. Moody's meetings. It was held in a theater packed with a most select audience. There were noblemen and noblewomen, and a prominent member of the royal family was in the royal box.

Mr. Moody arose to read Luke 4:27: "And many lepers were in Israel in the time of Eliseus the prophet," but he stammered when he came to the name Eliseus. He went back to the beginning of the verse and read it again, but again he could not pronounce that name. He went back a third time, and still he couldn't pronounce it.

He closed the Bible and with deep emotion said, "O God, use this stammering tongue to preach Christ crucified to these people."

The power of God came upon him, and the whole audience was melted by the power of God. Those who heard him before and after that night said that they never heard him pour out his soul in such a torrent of eloquence as he did that night.

It will be a new day in our Christian service when we simply do what Mr. Moody did and ask God to bring His Spirit to our work, to our efforts, to our labor.

Jesus also connects perseverance with prayer. "Men ought always to pray"—that's the prayer. "And not to faint"—that's the perseverance.

When you think you cannot take one more step—you've taught your last Sunday school class, passed your last offering plate, preached your last message, driven your last church bus—the answer is prayer, for when you pray you always persevere.

I have displayed this statement in a prominent place in my office: Every person, saved or unsaved, ought to know a Spirit-filled person. Are you one?

8
It's Time to Secure Our Tools

"And the sons of the prophets said unto Elisha, Behold now, the place where we dwell with thee is too strait for us.

"Let us go, we pray thee, unto Jordan, and take thence every man a beam, and let us make us a place there, where we may dwell. And he answered, Go ye.

"And one said, Be content, I pray thee, and go with thy servants. And he answered, I will go.

"So he went with them. And when they came to Jordan, they cut down wood.

"But as one was felling a beam, the axe head fell into the water: and he cried, and said, Alas, master! for it was borrowed.

"And the man of God said, Where fell it? And he shewed him the place. And he cut down a stick, and cast it in thither; and the iron did swim.

"Therefore said he, Take it up to thee. And he put out his hand, and took it."—II Kings 6:1–7.

You'll notice that these "Bible college students" say to the founder and president of their school, "The place where we dwell with thee is too strait for us."

Isn't that just like Bible college students to complain about the rules and regulations?

But look back at verse 5: "But as one was felling a beam, the axe head fell into the water: and he cried, and said, Alas, master! for it was borrowed." Let's look at that seven-word phrase: "The axe head fell into the water."

Today, many believers are attempting to accomplish great things for God without the godly tools they once had. What use to a carpenter is a saw without the blade; what use to a master artist is a palette without the paint; what use to an author is a pen without the ink? Scriptural tools will always make spiritual tasks more successful.

In the Book of II Kings, chapter 6, we find the prophet Elisha causing the iron to swim. Of course that would not happen naturally, but we have a supernatural God. If the Bible says that the iron swam, the iron *did* swim.

This is only one of several miraculous occurrences in the chapter, including:

> Doing the impossible—vss. 1–7
> Knowing the unknowable—vss. 8–12
> Seeing the invisible—vss. 13–17
> Accomplishing the unthinkable—vss. 18–23

While reading this account of doing the impossible, we come across one of the most needful verses in the entire Bible. At first glance maybe you wouldn't notice it—verse 5: "But as one was felling a beam, the axe head fell into the water: and he cried, and said, Alas, master! for it was borrowed."

A well-known Bible student of another century once wrote about our text: "The narrative suggests that the accomplishment of the great works of the world depends very much upon keeping little things in working order." He went on to write, "A great victory may be lost by the snapping of the linchpin of an artillery wheel. The sons of the prophet could not raise a house to the honor of God without the help of an ax." And then that great Bible student of another day tied up his thoughts by saying, "Great weights hang on small wires."

Never forget that the scriptural snapshot of the young prophet striving to build a Bible college dormitory without the ax head yesterday is also the sad snapshot of the earnest believer that is striving to build upon the kingdom of God without the ax head today.

Those of us who are saved can lose those imperative things that give us the cutting edge in our efforts for the Lord Jesus Christ.

It is possible to be working for the Lord and be in His will without having the cutting edge. It is very probable that some Christians sing in the choir, some preachers preach in the church, some bus workers run a Sunday school bus or someone works in the nursery while still missing the cutting edge.

I want to mention three important ax heads, the loss of which can impede believers in their labor for the Lord.

I. A Personal Testimony

"And Stephen, full of faith and power, did great wonders and miracles among the people."—Acts 6:8.

91

A believer's labor will be impeded if he loses the important ax head of his personal testimony.

The physician Luke tells us of the outstanding reputation of the respected and reverent deacon Stephen. The words that were attached to his name in and out of the early church were "full of faith," "power" and "great wonders and miracles." Even among the first seven table waiters, it is immediately very clear that he stands heads and shoulders above the rest.

It is interesting to note that Stephen's stellar testimony in the world got him a scriptural task in the church. And that should be the way it works. Your testimony in the world opens doors for you in the church.

The Bible says in Acts 6:5, "The whole multitude...chose Stephen, a man full of faith and of the Holy Ghost."

T. DeWitt Talmage, my favorite preacher of the past to read after, must have had someone like Brother Stephen in mind, when he wrote, "The mightiest influence for good on earth is a consistent Christian." He went on to pen, "I like the Bible folded between lids of cloth or calfskin, but I like it better when, in the shape of a man, it goes into the world a Bible illustrated."

The Bible says, "Let your light so shine before men, that they may see your good works, and glorify your Father which is in heaven" (Matt. 5:16). The Christian who pays little or no attention to his attitudes, words, destinations, hobbies, clothes, allegiances, colleagues and passions has probably put out the only light that would have gotten his unsaved family and friends and fellow workers to the safe, eternal shores of Heaven.

D. L. Moody used to tell of a ship that was caught in a storm on Lake Erie. This ship was trying to make the Cleveland harbor. The entrance to that port had what they called the upper lights (way back in the bluffs, brightly burning) and the lower lights (showing the entrance). But when the ship came near the harbor, they could not see the lower lights showing the entrance to the port. Someone had neglected the lower lights, and they had gone out.

The pilot said that they'd better get back on the lake again, but the captain said that they would go down if they did. The pilot said that there was very little hope of making the harbor; if he had nothing to guide him, he could not steer the ship on course. The captain insisted, so they tried all they could to get in. The vessel was dashed to pieces, and many lives were lost.

With great pathos in his voice, Mr. Moody said, "Let us take warning. God keeps the upper lights burning as brightly as ever, but He has left us down here to keep the lower lights burning."

Christians, we need to take the words of P. P. Bliss' hymn that came from that moving illustration as the theme for our lives:

> Trim your feeble lamp, my brother;
> Some poor sailor tempest-tossed
> Trying now to make the harbor
> In the darkness may be lost.
> Let the lower lights be burning!
> Send a gleam across the wave!
> Some poor fainting, struggling seaman
> You may rescue, you may save.

We lose our ax head when we've lost our personal testimony.

II. A Prevailing Triumph

"Nay, in all these things we are more than conquerors through him that loved us."—Rom. 8:37.

A believer's labor will also be impeded if he loses the ax head of a prevailing triumph.

The word *prevailing* means "to have superior force or influence." Paul tells us that believers are always much more than winners because of the love of Christ, in spite of the circumstances and conditions in which they find themselves.

I'm neither boasting nor bragging, but I am a winner. And if you are a child of God, you are a winner as well.

I was preaching in a tent meeting in the inner city where we had over three hundred people saved. One night I walked under the tent and was met by one of the men in the church. I said, "Hello, brother, how are you?"

You know, there are times when it is a mistake to ask that question, and this was one of them. Years ago I was having a meal with a preacher who was still bemoaning the fact that he had lost a church family thirty years before! I was tempted to say, "Here is the tissue, 'cause it looks like you have an issue!"

This man under the tent said, "To be real honest with you, Dr. Hamblin, I am discontented."

Over three hundred people were saved, there was

great Bible preaching, we heard wonderful songs of Zion, and this man was discontented! And he absolutely acted like someone had taken Romans 8:37 out of his Bible and stolen his all-day sucker.

We need to understand that our labor for the Lord Jesus Christ will be impeded if we lose the important ax head of prevailing triumph.

When someone said to Dr. Tom Malone, "I'm doing well under the circumstances," he would say, "What are you doing under there?"

When we lose a prevailing triumph, we have lost our ax head and are ineffective in the work of God.

There are several great things that will give the child of God the conqueror's mind-set.

1. The blood. "And they overcame him by the blood of the Lamb, and by the word of their testimony" (Rev. 12:11).

We do not need a Master's green golf jacket or a NASCAR trophy or a Hollywood Oscar or an NBA championship ring to be somebody. We are somebody when we've been to that "fountain filled with blood drawn from Immanuel's veins; [for] sinners plunged beneath that flood lose all their guilty stains." Then we are somebody!

What will give us a conqueror's mind-set is realizing that we've been washed in the blood of the crucified One.

2. The Book. "Thy word is a lamp unto my feet, and a light unto my path" (Ps. 119:105).

Whenever you see a believer holding a King James

Bible, you are looking at somebody who, no matter how dark the hour, has a lamp for his soul and a light for his sojourn. How can you carry God's Word and still be depressed? How can you be despondent? How can you be discouraged? God's Word makes it a spiritual impossibility!

3. The blessed hope. "Looking for that blessed hope, and the glorious appearing of the great God and our Saviour Jesus Christ"(Titus 2:13).

No matter how things may look around the Christian, if he would for a moment fix his eyes upon the sky, he would be moved by the truth that he could be headed in that same direction at any second.

One day we'll hear a toot and then we'll scoot! We'll hear a shout and then we're out! We'll hear the trump and then we'll jump!

We ought to revel in the fact that the next event on God's prophetic program is the rapture. It could happen before you finish reading this sermon, before the sun sets tonight. The Lord is coming, and that ought to give you a conqueror's mind-set, because you can't whine and whimper and belly-ache and bemoan when you know about the blood, the Book and the blessed hope.

It is high time that the people of God started carrying themselves like they are somebody. This idea that we are to be beat up and beaten down, that we're to crawl from point *A* to point *B*, is just absolutely foreign to the Word of God. The last time I checked, we're on the winning side. The last time I checked, we're ahead by ten, the game's almost over, and we've got the ball.

Oh, that every child of God would realize that the three great things that will give him a conqueror's mind-set are the blood, the Book and the blessed hope.

There come from the old and forgotten pages of church history many spiritual giants of past generations. Without question one of those individuals was John Bunyan. He was born in Elstow, Bedfordshire County, England in 1628. In 1660 Sir Francis Wingate learned that Bunyan was intending to preach near the small village over at Lower Samsell and issued a warrant for his arrest. Bunyan might have easily escaped, but he felt it was his duty to preach. In the midst of the service, the constable entered and arrested him.

The next day before Judge Wingate, he was charged with preaching without a license. Bunyan was taken from Wingate's court to Bedford's jail. For the next twelve long years he served out his sentence separated from his family and fellow believers.

Knowing of his great love for his family, including his blind daughter, the authorities at his trial told him he could go free if he would promise not to preach again. Although he knew the pain of separation would continue, Bunyan told the court, "If I am released today, I will preach tomorrow."

While unfairly and unjustly in prison, John Bunyan, with a Bible in his hands—it was not the NIV (non-inspired version), not an RSV (really spurious version); it was a King James Bible—and a conqueror's mind-set in his heart penned *The Pilgrim's Progress*, a Christian classic that, next to the Bible, has been read by more people than any other book. It was not written at an exclusive inn; it was written in a dirty jail.

Because Brother Bunyan—through prevailing triumph—didn't allow a dungeon to get him down, the church has the classic book that has blessed and benefited countless Christians.

III. A Powerful Touch

"And when he [the Lord incarnate] *saw that he prevailed not against him* [Jacob], *he touched the hollow of his thigh; and the hollow of Jacob's thigh was out of joint, as he wrestled with him."*—Gen. 32:25.

Finally, the believer's labor for the Lord will be impeded if he loses the important ax head of a powerful touch.

The prophet Moses tells us of that middle-of-the-night encounter that Jacob had with the angel of the Lord. I believe that that angel of the Lord was the pre-incarnate Christ. This was the most important event of Jacob's existence, and it happened at night when he was alone, when it seemed like his world was coming apart. But this encounter would literally transform and take his life to another level of spiritual usefulness.

It was at Peniel, meaning "facing God," that the touch of omnipotence came and the name Jacob, meaning "supplanter," was changed to "Israel," meaning "a prince of God." Thus the truth is conveyed that if a believer will seek the face of God, submit to emptying of self, secure the touch of Heaven and stop supplanting, he will succeed as "a prince of God."

But all this revolves around "he [God] touched the hollow of his [Jacob's] thigh."

If we lose the ax head of a powerful touch, it will

impede our labor for the Lord Jesus Christ.

Ephesians 3:20 says, "Now unto him that is able to do exceeding abundantly above all that we ask or think, according to the power that worketh in us."

The grievous sin that is being committed in our fundamental circles is the tendency to try and get by, get through and get along by our education, by our excellence, by our excitement and by our eloquence.

Do not misunderstand me; I am for education—I am thankful that I am closely connected to the Midwestern Baptist College—but education cannot take the place of enduement.

I am for excellence; if there is anything outside the power of God we need in the work of God, it is excellence. We need to quit this sloppy, sluggard mind-set; if it's for the Saviour, it ought to be sharp, first-class and the best we can do!

Many times I have preached in churches where the secretary has come and shown me their revival flyer that has one or more mistakes: the church address is incorrect, the service times are a.m. instead of p.m., the ad on the back for Vacation Bible School is antiquated, and—this is really important—they've misspelled my name! Our work for the Lord ought to be *topnotch;* it ought to be *sharp*; it ought to be *polished*. Our work should not be held together with rusty wires and duct tape. I am for excellence, but excellence cannot take the place of an enduement.

I'm for excitement! I'm not trying to be harsh—God knows my heart—but I know some preachers who need a transfusion of excitement. God deliver us from preachers who, when they preach, cannot be heard past the second row! God deliver us from preachers who, when they preach, sound like SpongeBob SquarePants!

When Dr. Malone was the pastor at the great Emmanuel Baptist Church a number of years ago, he had me in to preach. When I preach, I preach according to Scripture: "In the sweat of thy face shalt thou eat bread" (Gen. 3:19); and I had just finished preaching and was just mopping my face when Dr. Malone walked up to me and started thumping me in the chest with two fingers. He said, "John, every time you preach, preach like you preached tonight!" So if you're having trouble with my preaching, remember that it was Dr. Malone who encouraged me.

Abraham Lincoln said, "When I hear a man preach, I like to see him act as if he were fighting bees."

I am for excitement. One thing that would help many a preacher's sermon is sweat! But excitement cannot take the place of enduement of power. We can be in the work of God and in the will of God and absolutely going at it with chips flying and still be ineffective in our service because we have lost the ax head of a powerful touch. There is no substitute for an enduement of power.

I am for eloquence. As a preacher, words are my tools, but eloquence is not a substitute for enduement.

In February 2003, Dr. Malone and I were in Murfreesboro, Tennessee. We spent two full days working on two book projects—his book entitled *Tom Malone: "The Preacher From Pontiac"*, and my book entitled *Fire in the Pulpit*. On Saturday afternoon we flew out of Nashville airport. Neither of us had passed out business cards or carried on loud conversations with each other, but at the end of the flight one of the stewardesses came to me and said, "Are you two preachers?" I told her we were, and then I asked her how she knew. She said, "Several reasons: one, because you were both polite with each other; two, by the way you interacted with each other; three, you treated each other with the highest respect."

Let me add here what Dr. Bob Jones, Sr., used to say: "If anyone ought to be a gentleman, it is a saved man. And if anyone ought to be a lady, it is a saved woman." Being rude and crude is foreign to the Bible! For some reason, we have gotten the idea that everything that comes out of our mouth should be witty, when most of the time it is stupid.

Then she said, "I knew you were preachers because as soon as the plane took off, the older gentleman pulled out his Bible. I looked over his shoulder, and he was in the Book of II Corinthians. And you pulled out your briefcase, and you began to do some work. Neither one of you wasted any time on the flight." Then tears welled up in her eyes, and she said, "I really knew you were preachers when you two stepped on this plane and the whole atmosphere of the cabin changed and I sensed the power of God. I've been around the power of God enough to know when somebody has it."

We ought to have a powerful touch. If we lose this ax head, we've lost one of the most vital ax heads. Dr. Tom Malone never lost that ax head, and he set a standard for many of us to follow.

Back to II Kings, chapter 6. They were building a college, and in the midst of cutting wood, the most important part of an instrument was gone. The Bible college student said, "I've lost the ax head." How many could say with that young man, "I've lost the ax head of a personal testimony! I've lost the ax head of prevailing triumph! I've lost the ax head of a powerful touch! Oh, I need to get it back!"

"And the man of God said, Where fell it? And he shewed him the place."

If you've lost your ax head, ask the Lord now to restore and repair it.

9
It's Soul-Winning Time

"The fruit of the righteous is a tree of life; and he that winneth souls is wise."—Prov. 11:30.

The Bible presents a strong case for the Christian to become a capable soul winner. Witnessing, evangelism and soul winning are pronounced on almost every page. It is from the Word of God that the saved individual is called upon to be a consistent soul winner.

The Book of Proverbs is one of the books that is classified as the poetry of Scripture. Job, Psalms, Proverbs, Ecclesiastes and Song of Solomon all belong in the same package because they are written as Hebrew poetry. This twentieth book of the Bible is sometimes called "the Proverbs of Solomon," since that wise king wrote most of its wise sayings.

King Solomon composed 3,000 pithy statements. "And he spake three thousand proverbs: and his songs were a thousand and five" (I Kings 4:32). But the wisest thing Solomon was ever inspired of the Holy Spirit to write is our text, for it deals entirely with personal work.

"The fruit of the righteous is a tree of life; and he that winneth souls is wise." The word "wise" means "to be intelligent, skillful or artful." When Christians become soul winners, they become intelligent, skillful and artful in the eyes of God.

As a believer, as a child of God, as a Christian, we are either soul winners, or we are backsliders. He wants us to be soul winners, and that should be the very thing on which we spend our energies and efforts.

There are three Bible reasons—and there is no better reason than a Bible reason—that a believer should be a soul winner.

I. The Example of Jesus

"There cometh a woman of Samaria to draw water: Jesus saith unto her, Give me to drink."—John 4:7.

Jesus Christ initiated a conversation with a woman which resulted in her conversion. In the city of Sychar, this woman was known as the town tart and home-wrecker. She had deliberately gone to Jacob's well at noon, the hottest part of the day, so she wouldn't be seen and wouldn't have to speak to anyone.

A well-known Bible scholar once penned, "Jesus saw a potential child of the Highest. It was therefore in keeping with the ideals of His ministry that He should make special effort to reach this outcast."

It was while sitting on the side of a well curb at high noon that Jesus tenderly, truthfully and tactfully won this woman to Himself.

God is not only interested in those who are *down and out;* He is interested in those who are *up and out* as well. It doesn't matter if it is one engaged in prostitution or one with a position, a dealer of drugs or a dealer of diamonds; God is in the business of meeting people at the point of their need. And you and I that are saved must be soul winners because of the example of Jesus.

The Bible says, "For even hereunto were ye called: because Christ also suffered for us, leaving us an example, that ye should follow his steps" (I Pet. 2:21).

If you trace the footsteps of Jesus, you will discover that they always lead to an unsaved family member, a lost plant foreman and an unsaved neighbor. When your footsteps are falling in His footprints, every single time, without exception, you will be heading toward someone who knows not the Lord.

Once as we arrived at a service where I preached this message, I was getting out my Bible and putting on my preaching jacket when I turned around to say something to my wife. She was already headed across the parking lot to three fellows who were sitting on a curb to give them three gospel tracts. She was putting her footsteps inside the footprints of Jesus, for when she goes after a lost soul, she is following His example.

Several years ago our country was introduced to the WWJD craze—it was on bracelets, T-shirts, bumper stickers; it was everywhere, including cigarette cases and alcoholic cup holders. WWJD—what would Jesus do? Friend, He would head for someone either in His family or somebody else's family who was lost and needed to be saved—that's what Jesus would do!

Before one of the great battles of the Civil War, General Robert E. Lee, perhaps personally beloved of his armies more than any other military leader, went out to visit the encampment of some of his most hard-pressed companies. The tired men formed and stood at attention as he, on his famous white horse, walked slowly before the ranks. There was utter silence as every man saluted.

Then General Lee rode back along the line. Speaking not a word, but with the dignity that never left him, he took off his hat, bowed slightly and then rode slowly away.

Suddenly a Georgian sergeant could not contain himself any longer. He burst out of the ranks and shouted to the men, "Now then, after what the general has said, will you fight or won't you?"

Now then, Christian, after what Jesus has said, will you be a soul winner or won't you?

II. The Emphasis of the Early Church

"And they, continuing daily with one accord...with gladness and singleness of heart,

"Praising God, and having favour with all the people. And the Lord added to the church daily such as should be saved."—Acts 2:46, 47.

God tells us how the primitive church had people saved, baptized and added to it every day. It is mind-boggling that every twenty-four hours there were people added to their assembly! We know what it is to have subtractions every twenty-four hours, but they had additions!

Mark it down, the heartbeat of the early church was soul winning. Unfortunately, there are many fundamental churches that have moved their emphasis from soul winning to suppers and singing.

There are three *G*s that are killing our fundamental churches:

1. Graham, Billy

2. Gaither, Bill—if you must close your eyes to get a blessing when someone sings, that is not somebody you ought to hear sing. People will go hear a Gaither concert but won't come to Sunday school. You can pack a house with groupies, but you can't get them to come to the house of God to hear the Word of God.

3. Gothard, Bill—people go off to these Gothard meetings, and they think those little red notebooks are Bibles and that the only preacher who knows anything is Gothard.

Some churches have moved the emphasis from soul winning to sports. I'm not preaching against sports; I enjoy sports. But for every one person who goes soul winning, there are ten who will come to a church-sponsored sports activity.

We should be soul winners because of the emphasis of the early church.

The Book of Acts is about the early church; it is about the ministry of the disciples; it is about the ministry of the local bodies.

There are three locations in the Book of Acts where the early Christians witnessed.

1. At the Synagogue. "And it came to pass in Iconium,

that they went both together into the synagogue of the Jews, and so spake, that a great multitude both of the Jews and also of the Greeks believed" (Acts 14:1).

Many times people who have *only* religion are very open to a relationship with the Lord Jesus Christ. They can have a ton of religion without having salvation. People don't go to Heaven because of a denomination; they go to Heaven because they are born again!

Dr. Ed Reese recently received a soul-winner's award. He shared with me a story about when he and his wife were traveling through New England. They got a motel room where you walk right from your car into the room. A car pulled up beside them as they were unloading their car, and two ladies got out dressed in black from head to foot. Dr. Reese walked up to them and gave one of them a gospel tract, and he found out that the woman to whom he was talking was celebrating her fiftieth anniversary as a nun.

He said, "Do you have any peace?"

Tears welled up in her eyes, and she said, "I have *no* peace. I have *no* comfort. I have *no* solace." And in less time than it takes for me to tell it, he took an open Bible, and in the parking lot of that motel won that nun to Christ.

2. At the Store. "Therefore disputed he in the synagogue with the Jews, and with the devout persons, and in the market daily with them that met with him" (Acts. 17:17).

You can tell the market cashier about Christ as you are paying for your cornflakes. When you're going through the express checkout line (which is not an express; instead of having twenty items, people have a hundred items with no labels on any of them), you can give him or her a gospel tract and say, "When you get a chance, read this, and it will answer any question you may have about time and eternity."

3. At the Sinner's Doorstep. "I kept back nothing that was profitable unto you, but have shewed you, and have taught you publickly, and from house to house"(Acts 20:20).

When you go to a stranger's door and share the Gospel with him, you are being just like the saints in the early church.

Oh, that every person reading this would imitate the believers in the Book of Acts and witness at the synagogue, at the store and at the sinner's doorstep.

D. L. Moody told of one day seeing a steel engraving that pleased him very much. He said, "I thought it was the finest thing I'd ever seen at the time, and I bought it. It was a picture of a man floundering in the water and clinging with both hands to the cross of refuge. But afterward I saw another picture that spoiled this one for me, for it was so much lovelier. It was a picture of a person coming out of the dark waters with one arm clinging to the cross and the other lifting someone else out of the angry waves."

It is the local church that is to be consistently lifting lost souls out of the angry waves.

III. The Existence of Hell

"If thy hand offend thee, cut it off: it is better for thee to enter into life maimed, than having two hands to go into hell,

109

into the fire that never shall be quenched."—Mark 9:43.

Not only is the believer to be a soul winner because of the example of Jesus and the emphasis of the early church, but also because of the existence of Hell.

Mark 9:43 tells us that Hell is such an awful place that it would be better for a person to sever his hand from his arm and go to Heaven than to have both hands and go to Hell.

It must be noted that these words fell from the lips of the Lord Jesus Christ, who was Himself a hellfire-and-brimstone Preacher. Any preacher worth his salt will be accused of being a hellfire-and-brimstone preacher. God deliver us from these preachers who preach from the Bible but never preach on Hell. God deliver us from these churches that say, "We don't want a preacher who preaches on Hell, because it is too negative and narrow."

I tell people I am as negative and narrow as my Bible; in fact, I am so narrow on Bible doctrine that I can look through a keyhole with both eyes!

Dr. Bob Jones, Sr., once said, "What this nation needs is about six months of preaching on Hell every day and twice on Sunday!"

Jesus tells us that Hell is a place of fire (Matt. 5:22); a place of darkness (8:12); a place of weeping (22:13); a place of memory (Luke 16:25); a place where you don't want your loved ones to go (vss. 27, 28). These verses make it crystal clear that Jesus preached on Hell, and we ought to be soul winners because of the existence of Hell. The doctrine of Hell ought to defrost the frozen hearts of Christians for lost souls.

Jude 23 says, "Others save with fear, pulling them out of the fire; hating even the garment spotted by the flesh."

If your family is not saved and they do not get saved, each one of them will spend eternity in Hell. If those with whom you work do not get saved, they will spend eternity in Hell. If your neighbors do not get saved, they will spend eternity in Hell. If the gas station attendant whom you see every week doesn't get saved, he'll spend eternity in Hell. If your mail carrier doesn't get saved, he or she will spend eternity in Hell. If that person who crossed your path today, whether or not you knew him personally, doesn't get saved, he'll spend eternity in Hell.

According to an article in the June 11, 1984, issue of *U.S. News & World Report*, a fire burned so fiercely in the abandoned coal shafts deep beneath Centralia, Pennsylvania that a man once fried six eggs over a hole near the Odd Fellows Cemetery.

The fire began in 1962 and is one of the scores of underground blazes that the Federal Office of Surface Mining estimates are burning out of control in more than a dozen states.

Though Centralia's surface is not much hotter than that of nearby towns, underground temperatures have exceeded 1,000 °F, which is hot enough to melt heat-resistant probes lowered through boreholes to gauge the fire.

I am told that because of these underground coal fires, in the wintertime the grass is green and the snow melts.

But there is a fire that has been burning much longer and much hotter than Centralia's fires, and it is the flames of Hell!

We've seen from the pages of the Bible why the believer should be a soul winner. When it comes to soul winning, we need to make it personal, for it is possible to go to a soul-winning church and still not be a soul winner. Each one of us needs to say, "Lord, use me. I want to have Your power and be an instrument in Your hand in the saving of precious souls."

We need to be soul winners, for "the fruit of the righteous is a tree of life; and he that winneth souls is wise" (Prov. 11:30).

10
It's Promotion Time

"And in those days, when the number of the disciples was multiplied, there arose a murmuring of the Grecians against the Hebrews, because their widows were neglected in the daily ministration.

"Then the twelve called the multitude of the disciples unto them, and said, It is not reason that we should leave the word of God, and serve tables.

"Wherefore, brethren, look ye out among you seven men of honest report, full of the Holy Ghost and wisdom, whom we may appoint over this business.

"But we will give ourselves continually to prayer, and to the ministry of the word.

"And the saying pleased the whole multitude: and they chose Stephen, a man full of faith and of the Holy Ghost, and Philip, and Prochorus, and Nicanor, and Timon, and Parmenas, and Nicolas a proselyte of Antioch:

"Whom they set before the apostles: and when they had prayed, they laid their hands on them.

"And the word of God increased; and the number of the disciples multiplied in Jerusalem greatly; and a great company of the priests were obedient to the faith.

"And Stephen, full of faith and power, did great wonders

and miracles among the people."—Acts 6:1–8.

It is absolutely amazing to study the vast difference between the world's method of success and Heaven's method of success. This difference is larger than the distance between the North Pole and the South Pole, which is over 12,000 miles. When someone attempts to advance in life man's way, he will end up at failure's hovel; but if he uses God's way, he will eventually turn up at fulfillment's palace.

Acts, chapter 6, shows us three stages of activity engaged in by the servants chosen by the church:

> Serving tables—vss. 1–7
> Doing wonders—vs. 8
> Facing enemies—vss. 9–15

While Stephen would become notable as the first martyr of the new church, Luke tells us that he was at first appointed to what many would call a meaningless job—serving tables: "Wherefore, brethren, look ye out among you seven men of honest report, full of the Holy Ghost and wisdom, whom we may appoint over this business."

The word "business" here describes that which is "necessary or needful." A well-known Bible student once wrote, "We commend the action of the apostles, for their preparation of sermons left little time to devote to the menial task of dispensing physical necessities. They were not willing to leave the important work of preaching and, therefore, urged other suitable men to be appointed to superintend the humbler activities of the church....The multitude chose Stephen, and the choice was admirable."

Stephen's life on the pages of the Holy Scriptures serves as an interesting study on the important subject of spiritual success. Christians can go from being the water boy to being the captain on God's wonderful team.

You would not be reading this sermon if it wasn't your desire or dream or drive to be a better Christian. We ought to want that.

We can go from the bottom to the top, from the back to the front, from the pantry to the pulpit. There are three set ways that the believer advances in the Word of God. "Set" means that they cannot be skipped, they cannot be sidestepped and they cannot be skated around.

I. Be a Servant

"...whom we may appoint over this business."—Acts 6:3.

The physician Luke tells us that the early church instituted an important position to eliminate an internal problem. A person can feel the full weight of verse 3 only when it is coupled with verse 2: "Then the twelve called the multitude of the disciples unto them, and said, It is not reason that we should leave the word of God, and serve tables."

Either the apostles could serve widows or study the Word. They wisely chose seven men—Stephen being one of them—to wait on widows so they could work in the Word.

It is necessary to mention that in the expression "serve tables," the word "serve" is the verb form of the noun from which we get the English word "deacon." So their job description was to "deacon" the tables. So we see that deacons were never intended to be bosses, bureaucrats or bullies, but busboys.

An unknown poet wrote:

> Find out what God would have thee do;
> Perform that service well,
> For what is great and what is small
> 'Tis only He can tell.

We can succeed in the work of God by being servants. "Whosoever will be great among you, shall be your minister: And whosoever of you will be the chiefest, shall be servant of all" (Mark 10:43, 44).

It is unfortunate that within the four walls of our fundamental churches there are Christians who think that they can be the choir director without ever having once sung in the choir; they can be Sunday school teachers without ever once sitting in the classroom; they can be the Sunday school bus director without ever once going out on churchwide visitation; they can be the pastor without ever preaching in nursing homes, junior church or in the rescue mission.

If we are going to go from the back to the front, from the bottom to the top, from the pantry to the pulpit, then we have to become servants.

I am neither a prophet nor the son of a prophet, but I can tell you which students at our Bible colleges are going to make it in the ministry. Those who become successful are not the ones who hang out in the foyer, in the lobby, in the vestibule of the dormitory staring at their girlfriends. They are going to be washouts; they will wipeout; they will waffle when they finally graduate. But the ones who clean the restrooms, the ones who ask what they can do to help, they are the ones that will make it as preachers. When I see college boys helping to set up tables for a meeting and helping with last-minute things, I think, *Those young men are the next Spurgeons, Sundays, Talmages, Torreys and Malones.* They are servants!

A woman who was getting up in years was having trouble walking. She wanted to serve the Lord, and, although she couldn't get around well, she was able to play the piano. So she put an ad in the local newspaper: "Pianist will play hymns by phone daily for those who are sick and despondent. This service is free." And she included her phone number. When people called, she would ask which hymn they wanted her to play. Within a few months, she had played for several hundred depressed and lonely individuals. Frequently they would pour out their hearts to her, and she was able to encourage them. Later she testified that that service became the most rewarding thing she had ever done in her life.

If you are taking piano lessons today, you may be able to help someone spiritually tomorrow. Be a servant.

II. Be in the Shadows

"And the saying pleased the whole multitude: and they chose Stephen, a man full of faith and of the Holy Ghost, and Philip, and Prochorus, and Nicanor, and Timon, and Parmenas, and Nicolas a proselyte of Antioch."—Acts 6: 5.

Stephen was only one of the seven believers selected for this new spiritual slot, only one person on the list, but he soon began to rise to the top.

117

We will never rise to the top of the list until we are content to be just a name on the list of God's servants. Too many children of God seek the attention, applause and admiration as superstars for God. They do not realize that they can't have their own baseball card until they've been in a number of minor league team photos.

Young preachers often say to me, "I want to be an evangelist." Some of them can't even spell it! Some of them want the accolades that they think come with the title. Before you can be an evangelist, you need to have some dark places, some *nowhere* times on the "backside of the desert;" you cannot go to the top without having been in the shadows.

The dark places will do several things for the believer.

1. It builds character. "Moses kept the flock of Jethro his father in law, the priest of Midian: and he led the flock to the backside of the desert, and came to the mountain of God, even to Horeb" (Exod. 3:1).

Moses didn't have a flock of his own, but keeping his father-in-law's flock on the backside of the desert showed Heaven that Moses was ready to move to the mountain of God.

Don't *be* a character; *get* some character. Midwestern Baptist College, where I attended, strives to be a character-building factory.

2. It brings credibility. "Elisha the son of Shaphat...poured water on the hands of Elijah" (II Kings 3:11).

Christians should not think that they deserve the ear of the people until they have poured water on the hands of the prophet of God.

Two weeks after I was saved in 1979, God called me to preach. I began to preach within thirty days of being saved, and I've been preaching ever since. But at the beginning, my father-in-law, Dr. Ed Reese, pulled me aside and said, "John, I know you want to be an evangelist, but when you're not out preaching, you need a ministry here, because if you can't help people here, you can't help people out there."

I say the same thing to all of you: If you can't do it here, you can't do it out there!

Dr. Reese said, "I'm going to give you a ministry here. I want you to be the Wednesday night song leader." I do not have a singing voice, so why would he give me that ministry? "You need to get some platform mannerisms," he said. "You need to learn to be comfortable in front of a crowd. You need something to do that will help you gain credibility when you preach."

Keep that bus route; it brings credibility. Stay with that Sunday school class; it brings credibility. Stay in the choir; it brings credibility. Keep that jail ministry; it brings credibility. Start in the dark places; they will bring you credibility.

3. It births communion. "Samuel said unto Jesse, Are here all thy children? And he said, There remaineth yet the youngest, and, behold, he keepeth the sheep. And Samuel said unto Jesse, Send and fetch him" (I Sam. 16:11).

When a Christian walks with God while keeping

the sheep, it is certain that he will later walk with God ruling the nation.

You say, "Oh, I'll walk with God when I become a pastor." No! "I'll walk with God when I'm an evangelist." No! "I'll walk with God when I have my picture on a missionary prayer card." No! If you put an unspiritual person in a spiritual position, what you have is a mess!

You need the dark places because they build character, they bring credibility and they birth communion with God!

I rejoiced when my mentor, Tom Malone, Sr., told a particular story about when he was a student at Bob Jones College in Cleveland, Tennessee. While there as a student, he was the school's night watchman, working for twenty-five cents an hour. His hours were from 10:00 p.m. until 2:25 a.m. Sometimes he'd also have to feed the boiler, so it was somewhere around 3:30 a.m. when he got to bed. He had to get back up at 6:30 a.m. in order to make his first class.

One night when he was making the rounds, checking all the doors on campus to be sure they were secure, he put his hand on a doorknob and heard voices inside. He opened the door, and in that little room was an impromptu prayer meeting with several men on their faces praying for revival, getting right with God and seeking a meeting of the Lord.

He stepped inside and closed the door, fell to his knees and joined that prayer meeting. As a result, for the next three days there were no classes, no lectures and no schedules at the college as revival literally reverberated and rolled back and forth across the campus. There were preaching and singing and people getting right with God!

Dr. Tom Malone, Sr.,—successful pastor, respected college founder and chancellor, world-renowned fundamental leader, world-read author, tremendous pulpiteer and the Elijah of our day—was the night watchman. He did not get in the light until he'd been in the shadows, and nobody ever gets in the light until he's been in the shadows.

III. Be a Soul Winner

"And Stephen, full of faith and power, did great wonders and miracles among the people."—Acts 6:8.

How do we go from the back to the front? How do we go from the bottom to the top? How do we go from the pantry to the pulpit? Be a soul winner!

Because of the spirit-filled teaching and preaching of Deacon Stephen, he begins to step ahead of the other deacons. "Stephen...did great wonders and miracles among the people." We learn in the Book of Acts that he is the first man other than an apostle who is said to have performed miracles.

The greatest of these supernatural acts was spiritual healing. Make no mistake about it, he didn't have people standing in a healing line. His door-to-door soul winning is what brought spiritual success to Stephen.

These so-called Christian television programs do not line up with the Bible. What you hear on so-called Christian radio programs does not line up with the Bible. If these so-called "faith healers"—they're really *fake healers*—have what they say they have, why don't they empty hospitals of the sick? Why don't they go to the nursing homes and cure the afflicted? Why don't they go to the mental wards and heal the patients' minds? Why don't they go to funeral homes and raise people from the dead? Because they are nothing more than *religious fakes and frauds.*

Because of Stephen's sidewalk soul winning being so effective, God allowed him to have a shot at a sacred desk.

> *"They cried out with a loud voice, and stopped their ears, and ran upon him with one accord,*
>
> *"And cast him* [Stephen] *out of the city, and stoned him: and the witnesses laid down their clothes at a young man's feet, whose name was Saul."*—Acts 7:57, 58.

I believe his soul-winning efforts resulted in the glorious conversion of the apostle Paul, the Moses of the New Testament.

Daniel 12:3 says, "They that be wise shall shine as the brightness of the firmament; and they that turn many to righteousness as the stars for ever and ever."

Awhile back I was flying for a fall revival meeting in Maryland. Since 9/11 you have to be at the Detroit Metropolitan Airport two hours earlier than your flight in order to get through security; that means that I am usually at the airport longer than I am on the airplane. So I take a list of phone calls I need to return and make good use of my time while I'm waiting to board.

The first name that I needed to call that Saturday afternoon was a deacon at my home church. Several days prior to my call, he had brought a friend to church who had gone forward at the invitation. This deacon took his Soul Winners' New Testament and started to witness to him, when suddenly the deacon started to have chest pains and perspire profusely. People wanted to take him to the hospital immediately, but he said, "I am doing something here that's a little more important than that. When I am done leading my friend to Christ, I'll go to the hospital." When they got up from the altar, an ambulance was waiting to take the deacon to the hospital. At the hospital they discovered that he was in full-blown cardiac arrest.

He was weak and could barely talk when I phoned his hospital room, so I talked to his wife. She said, "Dr. Hamblin, we almost lost him this morning, but he rallied, and he's now doing better."

I could hear him whispering in the background, "Tell him I had a new roommate last night. I couldn't get out of bed, but I witnessed to him through the curtain. About 3:30 this morning, I led him to Christ. Tell Doc I'm going to get as many as I can while I'm here."

One morning my phone rang, and I knew by the earliness of the hour it was not going to be good news. My wife told me that they had let the deacon go home the night before but he died early that morning.

The church was packed with eight-hundred-plus people for his Home-going service. His wife greeted me at the door, holding the tract that I wrote and passing them out to everyone that she thought might be lost; six people got saved that morning.

By being soul winners, we can go from the back to the front; we can go from the bottom to the top; we can go from the pantry to the pulpit!

123

If you say, "Soul winning doesn't work," or, "It worked in the twenties, but it doesn't work in this era," you're not working it.

Do you know who sparkles and soars and shines in God's galaxy of stars? Without question, it is those saints who have given themselves completely to telling sinners about the Saviour.

Shortly before his death, Dwight L. Moody preached from Daniel 12:3. He then boarded a train and went to Kansas City; there he passed away. His body was returned home, and they held his funeral in church. C. I. Scofield was the officiating preacher. He mounted the pulpit and preached from II Samuel about one of David's mighty men whose "hand clave unto the sword (23:10)."

On that cold, wintry, weekday afternoon, in the midst of that Home-going service, a ray of light came through a stained-glass window and rested on Mr. Moody's face. It so moved the preacher and the congregation that Dr. Scofield stopped and commented about Moody's last preached text: "They that be wise shall shine as the brightness of the firmament."

Before they lowered his casket into that gaping hole, suddenly the night's first star shone in the western sky. Again, everyone remembered Moody's last part of Daniel 12:3: "And they that turn many to righteousness [shall shine] as the stars for ever and ever."

If you want to achieve success, you must do three things: be a servant, be in the shadows, become a soul winner. If you do that, you will be promoted from the pantry to the pulpit.

11
There's Always Time
for Loyalty

It is a heartbreaking fact that the infidelity and disloyalty of today's unbelieving, ungodly world has found its way into Christian circles. If there ever was an individual that should be devoted, diehard and dedicated, it ought to be the person who claims to be a child of God.

The words *fidelity* and *loyalty* should be synonymous with Christianity. In the Scripture there is an amazing account in which the prophet Elijah is supernaturally translated to Heaven.

> "And it came to pass, when the LORD would take up Elijah into heaven by a whirlwind, that Elijah went with Elisha from Gilgal.
>
> "And Elijah said unto Elisha, Tarry here, I pray thee; for the LORD hath sent me to Beth-el. And Elisha said unto him, As the LORD liveth, and as thy soul liveth, I will not leave thee. So they went down to Beth-el.
>
> "And the sons of the prophets that were at Beth-el came

forth to Elisha, and said unto him, Knowest thou that the LORD *will take away thy master from thy head to day? And he said, Yea, I know it; hold ye your peace.*

"*And Elijah said unto him, Elisha, tarry here, I pray thee; for the* LORD *hath sent me to Jericho. And he said, As the* LORD *liveth, and as thy soul liveth, I will not leave thee. So they came to Jericho.*

"*And the sons of the prophets that were at Jericho came to Elisha, and said unto him, Knowest thou that the* LORD *will take away thy master from thy head to day? And he answered, Yea, I know it; hold ye your peace.*

"*And Elijah said unto him, Tarry, I pray thee, here; for the* LORD *hath sent me to Jordan. And he said, As the* LORD *liveth, and as thy soul liveth, I will not leave thee. And they two went on.*

"*And fifty men of the sons of the prophets went, and stood to view afar off: and they two stood by Jordan.*

"*And Elijah took his mantle, and wrapped it together, and smote the waters, and they were divided hither and thither, so that they two went over on dry ground.*"—II Kings 2:1–8.

This entire chapter describes the following characters:

The companion—Vss. 1–13
The spectators—Vss. 14, 15
The doers—Vss. 16–22
The mockers—Vss. 23–25

The intense devotion and unwavering steadfastness of Elisha toward his mentor are obviously in full focus. The famous Bible expositor G. Campbell Morgan wrote about this narrative: "The man upon whom this mantle had already been cast followed him loyally, determined to stand by him."

Three different times and in three different places (vss. 2, 4, 6), Elijah told Elisha to tarry, and at the same three times and in the same three places, Elisha answered him, "I will not leave thee." This five-word phrase trumpets boldly and loudly the commitment of loyalty. It is a proclamation that defines the man and determines his agenda. The word *loyalty* simply means "faithfulness to a person or a cause, to an ideal or a custom."

The faithfulness and loyalty exhibited by Brother Elisha should be a pattern for each of us. If there is anything we need today, it is loyalty. Loyalty in marriage! Loyalty to family! Loyalty to our commitments at work! Loyalty to our godly heritage! Loyalty to the Scripture! Loyalty to God Himself! Loyalty to Christ! Loyalty to our good church! Loyalty! In one of his famous quips of homespun wisdom, Bob Jones, Sr., said, "If you ain't loyal, you ain't nothing!"

As a Christian, your loyalties should be specifically focused. Just as Elisha was loyal to Elijah, you too need to be specific in your loyalties.

I. Be Loyal to the Master

"When Jesus therefore saw his mother, and the disciple standing by, whom he loved, he saith unto his mother, Woman, behold thy son!"—John 19:26.

John tells us that he was the only male believer that remained with Christ while He was on the cross. The phrase "and the disciple standing by" says a volume about John's faithfulness to the Lord Jesus Christ.

Elizabeth C. Clephane must have had this verse in mind when she penned the last stanza to her hymn, "Beneath the Cross of Jesus":

129

I take, O cross, thy shadow for my abiding place;
I ask no other sunshine than the sunshine of His face—
Content to let the world go by, to know no gain nor loss,
My sinful self my only shame, my glory all the cross!

You and I should be loyal to the Master. Hebrews 13:13 says, "Let us go forth therefore unto him without the camp, bearing his reproach." How often people say, "What camp are you in?" Whenever anyone poses that question, every Christian should answer, "I am in Christ's camp, for there is no better!"

The moment the believer determines to stand faithfully with Christ, he will march away from the encampment of the world, the flesh and the Devil. If you would just be honest enough to take off that halo from your head and stick it in your pocket, you could then see and admit that your enemies are the world, the flesh and the Devil.

Every day of the world you have problems with the world. Every day of the world you have problems with the flesh. Every day of the world you have problems with the Devil.

You say, "Well, not me!" I want to see you after the service so you can sign my Bible. When I get home, I'll open my Bible to the flyleaf where you signed it and put your life verse, and under your signature I'll write: The biggest liar I've ever met!

You have problems with the world, problems with the flesh and problems with the Devil. You can primp it, you can perfume it, you can powder it, but flesh is still flesh. You have problems with the flesh, but the moment that a believer determines to stand faithfully with Christ, he'll begin to say good-bye to the world and good-bye to the flesh and good-bye to the Devil.

I recently read the history of when the Spaniards were besieging the little town of Saint-Quentin on the frontiers of France. Its ramparts were in ruin, fever and famine were decimating its defenders, and treason existed among its terrified population. One day the Spaniards shot over the walls a shower of arrows to which were attached little slips of parchment promising the inhabitants that if they would surrender, their lives and property would be spared.

As his sole answer, the governor of the town took a piece of parchment and wrote on it, "We have a king." He tied it to a javelin and hurled it back into the camp of the enemy. There was his one answer to all their threats and inducements.

Christians, when the arrows of spiritual treason are flying over the wall of your heart, just throw back to the enemy the javelin of devotion with a note that says, "I have a King!"

We need to be loyal to the Master.

II. Be Loyal to Your Mate

"For this cause shall a man leave father and mother, and shall cleave to his wife: and they twain shall be one flesh?"— Matt. 19:5.

Jesus tells us in this verse that the marriage relationship should supersede any other human relationship. He also instructed that it was a divinely ordained union that ought not to be broken by human acts or decree.

It must be noted that these words fell from the lips of the sovereign Son of God. When Jesus was dealing with the great matter of marriage, from his omniscient, vast vocabulary He pulled out the word "cleave." In the Greek language it means to "glue to." It is my conviction that young couples should be given as a wedding present a tube of glue with Matthew 19:5 written on it!

There are several ways that a husband and wife can demonstrate fidelity to their spouse. Jot these down, because if you went to a marriage counselor, this would cost you about $75 an hour, and you wouldn't get all that I'm going to give you.

1. Be complimentary to your spouse. "A word spoken in due season, how good is it!" (Prov. 15:23). Your marriage would be turned around today if put-downs were replaced with praises.

Oh, how it grieves my heart to hear how husbands and wives talk about each other, both in and out of each other's presence. Husband, you gave her your name, and she now has the same last name as you. When you stand there and talk bad about her, whether in or out of her presence, the only person that looks bad is you! Be complimentary. You ought to *honor* your spouse and *love* your spouse and *respect* your spouse.

One time I heard a preacher tell the story of a grouchy husband who could never be pleased; he was never happy. One morning his wife got up early and decided she would do her best to make her husband happy.

She made a big breakfast: two eggs (one sunny-side up and one scrambled), country ham and bacon, sausage and hallelujah biscuits (that's the kind you can't get in a can). She even squeezed the oranges herself. When old Grouchy came into the kitchen, he smelled the aroma of the coffee, and he looked at the feast before him and said, "You scrambled the wrong egg!"

There are a lot of husbands like that.

2. Be considerate of your spouse. "Be ye kind one to another, tenderhearted, forgiving one another, even as God for Christ's sake hath forgiven you" (Eph. 4:32). Kindness ought to be a word that describes how you treat your spouse twenty-four hours a day. It's not just in public, but in private as well.

How many times did I see Dr. Malone open the door for his wife and carry her Bible! There was in their marriage a spirit of consideration, and that's the way it ought to be in every home too.

3. Be completely in love with your spouse. "My beloved is mine, and I am his" (Song of Sol. 2:16). No other person should hold a place in your heart like the person who wears your matching wedding band.

Sometimes a young couple goes to get married, and an older couple will say, "Marriage just isn't all that it's cracked up to be." What an encouraging word! They'll say, "Once you get off the honeymoon stage of it, you'll hate every second of it." They are not prophesying; they are testifying the way it is in their house.

Being married is a blast! I'm enjoying every second of it. Outside of being saved, getting married is the best thing that's ever happened to me. If I had to do it all over again, hallelujah! I'd do it all over again!

When my wife was a student at Midwestern, she was working on a bachelor's degree in sacred music. One semester she had Dr. Tom Malone for English literature.

During that same time I was teaching at Midwestern and was also a trustee of the college.

One day I was on my way out just as she was arriving. We were standing in the lobby, and as I started to leave, I gave her a big kiss. Just about that time Dr. Malone walked in. He walked over to my wife and said, "Good morning, Cari." He then looked at me and said, "John, that's ten demerits." I thought, *Here I am a professor and a trustee of the college as well, and a student—my wife—didn't get zilch while I got hit with ten!* I pulled my wife close and I said, "Sweetheart, if we get ten, we might as well get a hundred!"

Be completely in love with your spouse. Oh, that every husband and every wife reading this would demonstrate fidelity to their own spouse by being complimentary, by being considerate and by being completely in love with them.

The greatest picture of loyalty I've ever witnessed between a husband and wife would have to be the devotion of Samuel Clay toward his ill wife, Delores. Brother Clay is a Bible deacon at a fundamental church where I have preached. A Bible deacon is a deacon that loves God, loves the man of God and loves the work of God. By the way, a Bible deacon is not the pastor's or the church's boss; he is a servant of servants—that's a Bible deacon.

Brother Clay and his wife were happily married for forty-six years. Mrs. Clay is now with the Lord, but when she had a serious heart attack and slipped into a deep coma, her husband took care of her. She was in a nursing home for three long years, and her husband was with her at all hours of the day and night taking care of her, combing her hair, washing her face, exercising her hands and carrying on conversations with her the same as you and I would carry on a conversation. That dear Christian man never wavered from his care for his wife. He never became bitter toward God.

The next time you and your spouse have a spat and you think about separation, I hope that you will remember Samuel and Delores Clay.

III. Be Loyal to the Man of God

"Only Luke is with me. Take Mark, and bring him with thee: for he is profitable to me for the ministry."— II Tim. 4:11.

The apostle Paul tells us that Dr. Luke was the only believer and fellow laborer who stayed by his side as he awaited certain martyrdom.

He was the greatest Christian who ever lived, the greatest preacher (outside of Jesus Christ) who ever lived, the greatest encourager of the people of God who ever lived, but when he came down to his dying days, only Luke was with him.

That's almost enough to make a stone weep. Think about all the people that Paul won to the Lord, all the Christians he instructed and encouraged in the way of God, all the people whose lives were influenced and impacted by his life; but when it came time for him to move from this world into another world, only one Christian was with him.

Everybody wants to be Paul, but nobody wants to be Luke. In those words, "Only Luke is with me," you find loyalty running over the brim! There is no way even to measure the tremendous degree of encouragement, peace and faith that Paul received by having Luke right there with him.

We don't know if they had any kind of conversation. I'm sure they did, though the Bible is silent on that, but all Paul had to do was look over at Luke, and he knew that somebody was in his corner.

One night a seven-year-old boy darted through the crowd and got my attention. He put a note in my hand, and when I got home later that night I opened the note. He had written a note of encouragement to me, and it made my heart glad.

Some of you think preachers don't need encouragement. I'll tell you what—we *do* need it! You say, "Well, you've got the Bible and a ministry and a degree and a position. You don't need encouragement from me." Listen! That's where you are sadly mistaken. Preachers are cut from the same bolt of cloth from which all Christians are cut.

That little boy's note was so special to me. I treasure it greatly.

The Bible says, "Remember them which have the rule over you" (Heb. 13:7). The Christian who is faithful to the pastor will do certain important things for him naturally. It's just like taking a step or a breath: you don't think about doing it; you just do it because those are things that happen naturally.

The faithful Christian will speak endearingly of his pastor's ministry. If I spent enough time with you, I could pretty much tell what you think of your pastor, because what is in the heart comes out of the mouth and what comes out of the mouth reveals what's in the heart. I don't have to be a theologian to figure that out.

The faithful Christian will support his pastor's leadership. You won't agree with every decision that is made, but you know who the pastor is. When I say "pastor," I use the singular and not the plural. If you think you can do a better job than your pastor, you should go down to your church and read the name of the pastor on the church sign. Then you should say, "Hallelujah!" because God knows what He is doing. Then go back home and support your pastor.

Our churches are literally filled with armchair pastors. These Monday-morning quarterbacks fantasize about how they would do it if they were the pastor, yet they have never preached one time in their lives. They wouldn't know hermeneutics from homiletics if they both stood in a row with name tags on them. They think they know everything though they themselves have done little.

Those that are faithful to a preacher will support his leadership. If you sense someone is not supporting your pastor, don't listen to him. Don't let your ears become garbage cans in which you allow them to deposit their gossipy trash. You tell them to take their garbage elsewhere.

At one church where I had not yet been a member for three months, I was out soul winning with a man with whom our pastor had paired me. We hadn't even gotten off the parking lot before this man began to criticize our preacher. I waited until he got all done, and then I looked at him and said, "Now, you can do one of two things. You can either tell the pastor what you just told me as soon as we get back to church, or you can wait until I tell him, because that's the first thing I'll do when I get back." Guess what? That's the last time anyone in the church ever criticized that pastor to me.

Those that are faithful to the pastor will stand by him until the last man. I hate negativity, but I would be less than honest with you if I told you that the work of God only has to do with people *coming*; it has to do with people *going* too. I've been told by sailors that when a ship begins to sink the first ones off are the rats, and I think you can make the application there.

Those that are faithful to the pastor will separate from all those who attempt to hurt his ministry. That means you don't eat with them. That means you don't talk to them on the phone unless you call to tell them, "Repent!" You separate from them.

If you are the kind of church member that will not separate from those who have attempted to hurt the ministry of your pastor, then I have one word that I want you to have ringing in your ears: DISLOYAL!

I'm not even going to have microwave popcorn with somebody that has tried to hurt a man of God. I'm not going to do it, and you ought to have the very same attitude.

King Henry VIII of England sent a delegation to the Vatican to seek to obtain from the pope a divorce from his first wife. The delegation was led by the Earl of Wiltshire. As was customary at the time, the Earl was expected to prostrate himself before the pope and kiss his toe, but he refused.

The story is told that he had taken along his dog (he was like many people are today; he never went anywhere without his pet). It is said that the dog went to the defense of his master. Instead of a kiss, the pope got a bite on his big toe! Hallelujah for that canine!

When it comes to the man of God, you should be just like the Earl of Wiltshire's dog—ready and willing to bite the toe of anyone who would attempt to hurt his ministry.

Isn't It About Time?

The text illustrates loyalty for us. The Bible repeatedly appeals to us to be loyal and show it. The Master, the Lord Jesus Christ, deserves your loyalty. Your spouse, the person with whom you exchanged "I *do*'s," deserves your loyalty. The man of God, the godly pastor of your good church, deserves your loyalty.

When Elisha vowed to Elijah, "I will not leave thee," he proclaimed his loyalty. Be loyal! Be loyal! Be loyal!

Oh, would to God the trait of loyalty be revived in our hearts. Isn't it about time for us to say to our Elijahs what Elisha of old said, "I will not leave thee"!

12
There Is a Time for Anger

"Now Elisha was fallen sick of his sickness whereof he died. And Joash the king of Israel came down unto him, and wept over his face, and said, O my father, my father, the chariot of Israel, and the horsemen thereof.

"And Elisha said unto him, Take bow and arrows. And he took unto him bow and arrows.

"And he said to the king of Israel, Put thine hand upon the bow. And he put his hand upon it: and Elisha put his hands upon the king's hands.

"And he said, Open the window eastward. And he opened it. Then Elisha said, Shoot. And he shot. And he said, The arrow of the LORD's deliverance, and the arrow of deliverance from Syria: for thou shalt smite the Syrians in Aphek, till thou have consumed them.

"And he said, Take the arrows. And he took them. And he said unto the king of Israel, Smite upon the ground. And he smote thrice, and stayed.

"And the man of God was wroth with him, and said, Thou shouldest have smitten five or six times; then hadst thou smitten Syria till thou hadst consumed it: whereas now thou shalt smite Syria but thrice."—II Kings 13:14–19.

141

Today in countless fundamental pews and pulpits, holy irritation is being replaced with unholy indifference. Instead of displaying militancy, many pulpiteers are becoming more and more like Milquetoast. The things that ruffled the feathers of our forefathers seem to be the very same things that people want to placate today.

In our text, we see the conclusion of the prophet Elisha's ministry. From his deathbed, Elisha directed King Joash to take a bow and arrows and to shoot one arrow eastward, then strike the ground with the arrows.

Because Joash had struck the ground only three times, he would strike down Syria only three times. If he had struck it five or six times, the threat of Syria would have been completely eliminated. Joash lacked perseverance and endurance.

If I have learned anything in over a quarter of a century of being in the Lord's work and crisscrossing the North American continent repeatedly, it is this: perseverance pays plenty when it is plugged into our work for God. I saw on one pastor's desk blotter this great manifesto: "For success in the ministry, preach, pray and plug away!" I recall hearing Dr. Curtis Hutson say, "The postage stamp is a success because it sticks to one thing."

If there is anything we need besides revival, the anointing of the Spirit of God and a spiritual awakening in the work of God, it is a new spirit of perseverance and endurance. The work of God is not a sprint; it is a marathon.

Because King Joash lacked perseverance and

endurance, the prophet Elisha became upset with him. This old, feeble and sickly man of God, though at death's door, became outraged: "And the man of God was wroth with him."

The word "wroth" means "to burst out in rage." Ephesians 4:26 is a New Testament sister verse of II Kings 13:19. It says, "Be ye angry, and sin not."

Martin Luther, the great Reformation leader, said, "I never work better than when I am inspired by anger, for when I am angry I can write, pray and preach well. Then my whole temperament is quickened, my understanding is sharpened, and all mundane vexations and temptations depart."

You and I should be like Brother Elisha of old and be incensed at the things we see taking place inside and outside of the house of God. Some things ought to upset us. Some things ought to make us "wroth." Oh, for God's people to have a revival of holy, righteous, Bible anger at what's going on today.

I want to mention three things that should infuriate the believer.

I. The Debasing of the Bible

"Now the serpent was more subtil than any beast of the field which the LORD God had made. And he said unto the woman, Yea, hath God said, Ye shall not eat of every tree of the garden?"—Gen. 3:1.

The word *debase* means "to corrupt or to pervert."

When Satan first appeared on the stage of Scripture, he made an insidious attack upon the Word of God. In a subtle, shrewd and skillful way he simply

143

put a question mark where God had placed a period.

Today's assault being waged against the Bible is not something that began in our lifetime; it is an assault that goes all the way back to the beginning of time in the Garden of Eden.

In reference to the Word of God, this world can be divided into two different groups: those who *commend* the Word of God and those who *corrupt* the Word of God. Every one of us can be placed in one category or the other.

"For we are not as many, which corrupt the word of God" (II Cor. 2:17). When such corruption shows itself, all of us should be infuriated. The debasing of the Bible should never be left unchallenged!

When you go to a so-called Christian bookstore and ask for a King James Bible, the salesperson has to push aside a statue of Mary, several strands of rosary beads and a variety of perverted versions of the Bible to get you a dust-covered KJV Bible.

Sending cards of encouragement is a fine thing for Christians to do. We all need to be encouraged. But when you receive a card of encouragement that has an inscribed verse from a sham Bible, what a disappointment!

What do you think when some preacher makes the blatant statement, "This verse is incorrect in the King James Version. It should read like this...."?

When such things happen, like Brother Elisha of old, we should become outraged! Do you get upset? Do you get angry when you witness the debasing of the Bible?

D. L. Moody, the greatly used evangelist of the nineteenth century, told about a man who took his own Bible to his liberal, Bible-denying, modernistic pastor and said, "This is *your* Bible."

"Why do you call it *my* Bible?" he asked.

"Because I've been sitting under your preaching for five years, and whenever you have said that a particular thing in the Bible was not authentic, I cut it out. *Your* Bible no longer contains the Books of Job, Ecclesiastes or Revelation, or a great deal more throughout the other books. This is *your* Bible!"

Dear Christian, don't you let anybody mess with *your* Bible. Don't let anybody tell you that even one particular thing is not authentic. Don't let anybody take anything out or put anything in *your* Bible. If they try, run away from them as fast as you can!

The debasing of the Bible ought to make us "wroth."

II. The Dividing of the Body

"Now I beseech you, brethren, by the name of our Lord Jesus Christ, that ye all speak the same thing, and that there be no divisions among you; but that ye be perfectly joined together in the same mind and in the same judgment."—I Cor. 1:10.

The apostle Paul pleaded with the believers in the church at Corinth to be at peace with one another. To feel the full impact of this verse, you must understand the definition of the word translated "beseech." It means "to entreat or to pray."

The Corinthian church was high on Paul's private prayer list. When I think of him 'beseeching' the brethren, I see him on his knees, tears streaming down his cheeks, pleading with them, 'Speak the same thing; don't allow division to come among you, but be perfectly joined together in the same mind and in the same judgment.'

Let me ask you some hard, searching questions.

How do you feel when a member of your church openly begins to play politics and rally and solicit an uprising against your pastor who has been true to his Saviour, the church and his call?

What comes to your heart when you pass a fundamental church that at one time was experiencing great growth, had a spirit of revival and was being blessed of God with mighty things, when you find that now it is not even a shadow of what it once was because of some satanically inspired troublemakers?

How do you feel when someone gets upset with your pastor and proceeds to take out his anger on the pastor's family?

I know it's hard to believe that people would get upset with someone as sweet and soft-spoken as I, but they do. That doesn't really bother me, because I'm preaching the Bible plainly as it is; but it does bother me when they don't have the courage to come directly to me and instead take it out on my wife and children. That is an outrage!

There are several things that will separate an assembly.

1. Personalities. "Now this I say, that every one of you saith, I am of Paul; and I of Apollos; and I of Cephas; and I of Christ. Is Christ divided? was Paul crucified for you? or were ye baptized in the name of Paul?" (I Cor. 1:12,13).

146

The only individual who should be preeminent in any church is the precious Saviour! It is not about anyone else.

2. Pride. "I wrote unto the church: but Diotrephes, who loveth to have the preeminence among them, receiveth us not" (III John 9).

Diotrephes' name means "nourished by Jupiter." Pride, whether it be on the inside or the outside of the house of God, is not nourished by God.

Pride keeps people away from the altar.

Pride keeps people out of the ministry. There are men who know beyond a shadow of a doubt that God has called them to preach, but they won't surrender, because that would be a bad business decision or it would interfere with their hobbies or they would be viewed as having a position of less influence in the community or in their family.

Pride keeps folks out of the choir. Some people can sing and shine in a solo or in a small group, but they'll not sing and shine with the other saints in the whole choir, because the spotlight is not on them.

Pride keeps Christians from getting right with one another. Staying right with others means you have to speak to a person with whom you're upset; you might have to accept some of the blame for whatever caused the problem; you might have to meet them more than half way.

Every Christian needs to hold a private funeral service for pride, bury it and then get on with serving God in harmony with others in the church.

We are going to spend eternity together, and if we can't get along within the four walls of our local church, it'll be a big adjustment getting along with those same folks when we meet them while strolling down Heaven's street.

If you can keep haughtiness out of a body, you can likely keep harmony in a body.

3. Petty problems. "I beseech Euodias, and beseech Syntyche, that they be of the same mind in the Lord" (Phil. 4:2).

Ninety-nine percent of all church difficulties are the result of petty problems. People get upset over the dumbest stuff, things that will not matter one whit in eternity.

In a meeting once I was commenting on Paul's statement to the Philippian jailer: "Believe on the Lord Jesus Christ, and thou shalt be saved, and thy house." I said, "Mr. Philippian Jailer got saved. Then Mrs. Jailer and all the little Jailers got saved." I went on to mention that if they had a dog or a gerbil or a parrot, they got saved too. A woman got upset with me because I didn't mention a cat. "And did you mean that their cat went to Hell?" This woman missed the entire meaning of the message because she was upset. The obvious fact that I did not mention her favorite animal is an absolutely petty matter.

"I've had to sit in the nursery three weeks in a row." Good for you! What a wonderful opportunity to serve the Lord by caring for His little lambs.

"I have to straighten up the church after the service and pick up all the trash people leave behind." What you really mean is you *get* to clean up the house of God and keep it straight for Him.

I feel sorry for folks who think it's a chore to read their Bible, to pray, to witness and to come to church on Sunday morning when they'd rather sleep in. The truth is they *get* to do these things for God and are *blessed* by reading the Bible, praying, witnessing and coming to church.

"The pastor didn't meet with a committee or have one meeting with the membership before changing the color scheme in the bathrooms!" Isn't that a tragedy? Be happy the bathroom is inside the building and the plumbing is working!

Some people have too much time on their hands. They get riled up and revved up about something silly that will not matter one iota in eternity.

I pray that every one of us could recognize that *personalities, pride* and *petty problems* will separate an assembly of believers and disrupt the ongoing work of God.

A visitor to a mental institution was astounded when he observed one lone man with only a small stick guarding one hundred inmates.

The visitor asked, "Aren't you afraid these inmates will get together and attack you?"

"No," replied the guard. "These people are here in the first place because of their inability to get their heads together and work cooperatively."

It will be a bad day for the kingdom of darkness when God's people in the local church get their hearts together and work cooperatively for the cause of Christ!

III. The Diluting of the Blood

"And almost all things are by the law purged with blood; and without shedding of blood is no remission."—Heb. 9:22.

The word *diluting* means "to weaken or reduce the force." The apostle Paul tells us that God places a divine emphasis upon the blood atonement of the Lord Jesus Christ. So enormous is the importance of this truth that the author of Hebrews does not step back from saying, "No bloody cross—no personal forgiveness."

If you don't have the cross, you don't have Bible salvation. If you don't have the blood, you don't have redemption.

I hear people say, "There are seven plans of salvation because there are seven dispensations." No! There is *only one plan of salvation* in the Bible.

The Old Testament sinner looked *forward* to the cross; the New Testament sinner looks *back* to the cross. Salvation is in the cross and nothing else. It is not by works, but by trusting in the finished work of Calvary. It is a blood-bought redemption; it is a blood-wrought salvation.

Some people do theological handstands and hermeneutical backflips, claiming that it was works in the Old Testament, that it is grace for us in the church age today, but that it will go back to works during the Great Tribulation. That is nowhere in the Bible!

The ribbon that runs from Genesis to Revelation is the blood. The river that runs from Genesis to Revelation is the blood. The road that runs from

Genesis to Revelation is the blood. It has never ever been by works, and it will never ever be by works!

Once when I was going to Ohio to preach in a church, I checked into the motel about 4:30 on Sunday morning. I gave the clerk a gospel tract and said, "I want you to read something I wrote; it's from the Bible." He thanked me for it.

Wednesday night I walked through the lobby on my way to the church to preach, and this same motel clerk was back on duty. He said, "Excuse me. I just want to give you some pointers on the gospel tract you wrote."

I said, "Okay."

He said, "I'm a graduate of a Church of Christ college. Your tract is adequate, but I notice that you did not mention baptism. You know, Dr. Hamblin, it is baptism that gets people to Heaven."

I said, "No sir, you are wrong, quite seriously mistaken! The road to Heaven is not a water route. You cannot swim to Heaven. There was no baptistry, no baptismal certificate and no baptismal robe at Calvary. The middle cross at Calvary is the only Way to Heaven—the crucified Son of God."

Jesus Himself said, "I am the way, the truth, and the life: no man cometh unto the Father, but by me" (John 14:6).

The blood of Christ is so important that no matter where you open the Bible, you will find a blood-stained page! It always has been and it always will be by the blood of the crucified One.

The third stanza of Elvina Hall's hymn "Jesus Paid

151

It All" is inspiring and instructive.

> For nothing good have I
> Whereby Thy grace to claim.
> I'll wash my garments white
> In the blood of Calv'ry's Lamb.
>
> Jesus paid it all;
> All to Him I owe.
> Sin had left a crimson stain;
> He washed it white as snow.

We ought to be infuriated at the diluting of the blood. The Bible says, "Unto him that loved us, and washed us from our sins in his own blood" (Rev. 1:5).

Let me ask you a couple of questions. Does your preacher preach on the blood of the Lord Jesus Christ? Some Christians sit under a so-called preacher who doesn't ever mention the blood of the Lord Jesus Christ even once in fifty-two weeks. Why do you not get out of that modernistic mausoleum? Because (you say) it's a family tradition to be a member of that church, and "Grandma is buried in the cemetery." Well, dig her up and move her—and move yourself as well!

What comes to your heart when the great hymns of the blood are shamelessly replaced with shallow musical ditties that never mention the atonement? There is a popular fallacy abroad today that says, "Throw out the hymnbook." Disliking the great music, these liberal rascals replace it with what Dr. Shelton Smith calls "7-11 music" which he defines as seven words repeated eleven times!

You cannot improve on John Newton's

> Amazing grace! How sweet the sound,
> That saved a wretch like me!

I once was lost but now am found;
Was blind, but now I see.

or Isaac Watts'

At the cross, at the cross, Where I first saw the light
And the burden of my heart rolled away.
It was there by faith I received my sight,
And now I am happy all the day!

or William Cowper's

There is a fountain filled with blood
Drawn from Immanuel's veins,
And sinners, plunged beneath that flood,
Lose all their guilty stains.

Since you're not going to improve on them, you should not try to replace them.

How do you feel when you see new converts carrying perverted versions of the Word of God that have either removed or altered the verses on the blood? When those things happen we, like Brother Elisha, ought to be "wroth"!

My preaching doesn't tell you anything new; it's the same as the preachers of old, except with cuff links. The fundamentalism that we have and enjoy has to be given to other generations coming behind us, and we must guard it and keep it pure as we give it to them.

We ought to make a big deal about the Bible. We ought to make a big deal out of the atonement. We ought to make a big deal about the church.

Other than a lifetime membership to a fitness club—which, by the way, makes only my wallet look slim and trim—the only other thing of which I am a member is my local church.

I am not against fellowship, but Jesus did not die for a fellowship, and He did not die for a home Bible study. Jesus died for His church, and that's where saved people ought to be members. Christians should belong to a local, fundamental, independent, Bible-believing, Bible-preaching, premillennial, soul-winning, missionary-minded church! There is nothing that can replace that!

If we're not cautious and careful, we'll coast along and *not* make a big deal out of the church. We'll let it be divided up and get involved with other organizations that are outside the authority and blessing of the church.

If we don't make a big deal about the Bible, the church and the blood, what will our grandchildren and great-grandchildren have when they go to church?

Several years ago a singing evangelist gave this testimony:

> I recently sang for a preacher whom I have known casually for over twenty years. I was astounded to hear him tell his adult Sunday school class, "The blood of Christ is not all that important, and Christians shouldn't make such a big deal about the atonement. It really doesn't matter how Jesus died, just as long as in some fashion He did."

But surely we all remember that the Bible says: "But if we walk in the light, as he is in the light, we have fellowship one with another, and the blood of Jesus Christ his Son cleanseth us from all sin" (I John 1:7).

The Bible I read tells me that there was a certain way in which Jesus had to die. It wasn't a haphazard event. It was on purpose and by the eternal and divine design of Almighty God. Very simply, He shed His blood for us.

You don't have Bible atonement or a legitimate salvation unless you have the cross and Christ's shed blood.

I once heard a so-called preacher say, "It doesn't matter how Jesus died. He could have died in His sleep between silk sheets. We still could have been saved." That is heresy! It's not Bible; it's total error! Jesus was true to the scarlet thread that runs throughout the Bible. He died according to the revealed plan of God clearly seen in the Bible.

Christians ought to be outraged and absolutely incensed. They too should be "wroth," yes, incredibly angry when someone, anyone dilutes the blood of the Lord Jesus Christ.

Like Brother Elisha of Old Testament fame, there are things about which you and I ought to be mightily upset: "And the man of God was wroth."

It is time to be angry if our anger is about the debasing of the Bible, the dividing of the body or the diluting of the blood.

13
It's Time to Stay Put

"But none of these things move me, neither count I my life dear unto myself, so that I might finish my course with joy, and the ministry, which I have received of the Lord Jesus, to testify the gospel of the grace of God."—Acts 20:24.

Many Christians today have the spiritual number for the moving truck in the front page of their spiritual phone directory. Unfortunately, some have even committed the digits to memory.

In the twentieth chapter of the Book of Acts, we find the apostle Paul's charge to the elders of Ephesus. In this chapter we find the following things:

> Paul's faithful companions—vss. 1–5
> Paul's final communion—vss. 6–12
> Paul's foolish concern—vss. 13–17
> Paul's farewell comments—vss. 18–38

In Paul's farewell comments, we read one of the most stirring and sobering verses in all of the Scriptures: "But none of these things move me, neither count I my life dear unto myself, so that I might finish my course with joy, and the ministry, which I have received of the Lord Jesus, to testify the gospel of the grace of God." Soon afterward Paul expressed the same sentiment in Acts 21:13: "Then Paul answered, What mean ye to weep and to break mine heart? for I am ready not to be bound only, but also to die at Jerusalem for the name of the Lord Jesus."

A well-known Bible student penned, "Paul's speech on the seashore at Miletus was probably the most pungent of all of his utterances."

The word "move" meant that the things that had happened to him were not going to determine his course of action. Christians should never permit what we went through yesterday to pack the moving truck today.

Far too many Christians seem to "move" and jump and go from one place to another in the moving truck all the time. If Jesus stays His coming, we are going to be tempted and tried and tested, and we'll think about getting the moving truck. But we need to be mindful of what Paul said: "But none of these things move me." So don't get the moving truck yet!

God has a will for every one of His children, not just the pastors or evangelists. In Acts, chapter 20, we find three things that kept Paul from being jerked or jarred out of the will of God.

I. Tears

"Serving the Lord with all humility of mind, and with many tears, and temptations, which befell me by the lying in wait of the Jews."—Acts 20:19.

158

1. Tears for the work. The physician Luke tells us that Paul served God with liquid emotion, with pathos, with a burdened and broken heart.

Note that Paul served Him with "all humility of mind." What is the work? It is singing in the choir, playing a church instrument, operating the sound system; it is being a deacon, a Sunday school teacher, a nursery worker—the work is whatever you do for God. Paul not only served, he had tears for the work.

2. Tears for the wicked. "Therefore watch, and remember, that by the space of three years I ceased not to warn every one night and day with tears" (vs. 31).

Within the city limits of each town in America there is a world that is dying and going to Hell. Somebody ought to have a burden; somebody ought to weep; somebody ought to have a broken heart for those that are unsaved.

A number of years ago I was witnessing to a teenager. When I asked, "Do you know Jesus?" he answered, "Who is Jesus?" Was there no one in that town with a broken heart or who had shed tears for the lost?

Dr. John R. Rice said, "Tears are the magnets that God uses to bring unsaved people to Christ."

Paul had tears for the work and for the wicked.

3. Tears for the workmen. "And when he [Paul] had thus spoken, he kneeled down, and prayed with them all. And they all wept sore, and fell on Paul's neck, and kissed him" (vss. 36, 37).

The workmen are the pastors, missionaries and

evangelists. We ought to have a special place in our heart for those who are the messengers of God, for those who are true-blue to the Lord, for those who every Sunday morning and night and every Wednesday night are delivering the message of God.

Paul wept for the work, he wept for the wicked and he wept for the workmen; and we should as well.

Sometime in this life, often many more times than once, we will drink from the cup of sorrow. Paul did, but he neither allowed tears to keep him from serving God nor cause him to leave the will of God.

Even a casual reading of the pages of the Word of God shows us that His great servants have always been burdened and brokenhearted about innumerable things, but they did not leave the will of God because of tears.

We are not to give up or quit, and we don't get the moving truck because of tears.

Awhile back I was preaching at the Sixth Avenue Baptist Church, which is in the heart of Brooklyn. It was started by Robert Lowry who was the hymn writer that wrote "Nothing But the Blood." He led Annie Hawks to Christ (she wrote "I Need Thee Every Hour") and baptized her in that church, and she joined it. This church is an historical landmark. It is over one hundred years old; R. A. Torrey and G. Campbell Morgan preached there, and I got to preach there!

Not far from the motel where I was staying was the Greenwood Cemetery. A number of famous people are buried there: Henry Ward Beecher, A. T. Pierson, T. DeWitt Talmage and Robert Lowry. J. C.

Penney, who was a Christian, and Samuel Morse, also a Christian and the man that invented the telegraph, are buried there.

Also in that cemetery is the grave of Ira Sankey. I stood by his grave and read his date of death, his wife's death and that of his son. There was one small headstone that had Hope Sankey on it. She was a daughter who was only four years old when she preceded her father in death.

I called Dr. Wayne Halleck and said, "I'm standing at the grave of Ira Sankey. Would you sing me a Sankey song?" He started singing "Trusting Jesus," and we had us a camp meeting as he sang

> Singing if my way is clear,
> Praying if the path be drear,
> If in danger for Him call,
> Trusting Jesus, that is all.

I thought of how Sankey must have stood there with his wife and son, and possibly with Moody, and how they mingled their tears together—but he didn't quit, he didn't give up and he didn't call the moving truck because of tears.

II. Temptations

"Serving the Lord with all humility of mind, and with many tears, and temptations, which befell me by the lying in wait of the Jews."—Acts 20:19.

Temptations did not move the apostle Paul out of the will of God. The physician Luke tells us that Paul was just like you and me. It absolutely thrills my soul to know that Paul was cut from the same bolt of cloth from which I'm cut.

He didn't say temptation; he said "many...temptations." That's plural, not singular. Paul did not allow "many...temptations" to move him from the will of God.

I want us to look at some things that will help us cope when temptations beset us, and all Christians have temptations in their lives.

1. God's example. "And when the devil had ended all the temptation, he departed from him for a season" (Luke 4:13).

In this passage, the Lord Jesus had just gone through the temptations in the wilderness. The Devil hit Him with temptation after temptation, and each time He was tested and tempted, the Lord gave the Devil a Bible verse. And each time He quoted the Bible, He got victory over the temptation. And then in verse 13, we find the *Devil leaving* and *Jesus staying;* the battle of temptation was decided with Jesus standing as the Victor!

That is God's example for us.

2. God's escape. "There hath no temptation taken you but such as is common to man: but God is faithful, who will not suffer you to be tempted above that ye are able; but will with the temptation also make a way to escape, that ye may be able to bear it" (I Cor. 10:13).

When I am standing in a pulpit, I can usually look out and see several exit signs. If the building caught on fire, there would be several escape routes; but if those exits were clogged and congested, we would be caught. God says that when temptation comes, He has built an exit, an escape; we do not have to succumb to temptation. There is an exit...if we look for it!

3. God's exhortation. "Watch and pray, that ye enter not into temptation: the spirit indeed is willing, but the flesh is weak" (Matt. 26:41).

The Lord says that we should "watch and pray" that we will not enter into temptation—that's His exhortation.

May every Christian realize that the things that will help him with serious temptations are God's example, God's escape and God's exhortation.

Peirasmus, the Greek word for "temptations" in Acts 20:19, means solicitations to do evil. Solicitation is an advertisement, but Paul says that though there were solicitations to do evil in his life, he (Paul) did not leave the will of God.

I saw a furniture commercial—a solicitation—on television that claimed you could get a whole truck-load of their furniture and not pay for it until the year 2015. I know this company's products, and, believe me, their furniture will not last that long. They are baiting you with a so-called bargain. Friend, you ought to be smart enough to know that when the Devil advertises something, no matter how big the bait, the bill is always bigger.

Don't get the moving truck yet because of temptation.

III. Testifying

"Testifying both to the Jews, and also to the Greeks, repentance toward God, and faith toward our Lord Jesus Christ."—Acts 20:21.

163

The physician Luke tells us that Paul witnessed to everybody. You couldn't be around him but that he would have a Bible verse, a gospel tract or an invitation to wherever he was preaching in that city. It was testifying that kept him from leaving the will of God.

How can we quit on God when we think about the last person we led to Christ? How can we quit on God when we think about the next person we want to lead to Christ?

The word "testifying" in the Greek is *diamarturomai,* meaning "to witness." This is what I call a golden nugget of truth from the gold mine in the Bible. Paul says, "I witnessed. I gave the Gospel. I testified both to the Jews and to the Greeks"—this is representative of the common people: the gas station attendant, the motel clerk, the grocery store cashier, the butcher, the baker and the candlestick maker.

But Paul's ministry does not stop in Acts, chapter 20. In fact, the Book of Acts closes with his "preaching the kingdom of God, and teaching those things which concern the Lord Jesus Christ, with all confidence, no man forbidding him" (28:31).

In the chapters between we see him witnessing to such people as King Agrippa. Wouldn't you like to witness to Agrippa? As the Jews and Greeks represent common people, so Agrippa represents an uncommon person.

The Bible says that "Christ should suffer, and that he should be the first that should rise from the dead, and should shew light unto the people, and to the Gentiles" (Acts 26:23).

We want to witness to King Agrippa, but you can't get to him until you witness to the Jews and the Greeks.

Billy Sunday said, "The most important work in the world is done by ordinary people." We need to keep witnessing to the common people.

Christianity is not about playing church or getting your way in church decisions; it is about keeping people out of Hell. That's what it is all about!

Many years ago I was holding a revival meeting in Annapolis, Maryland, the capital of the state. One night after the service the pastor and his family and several of us went out to eat at an all-night diner. Seated several tables away was a group of men who were sharply dressed and who seemed to carry themselves with an air of distinction and dignity with a professional polish about them. One of them looked very familiar to me. It turned out to be a liberal-to-the-bone senator.

The men at the table finished eating before we did, and as they passed our table, I said, "Mr. Senator, let me give you something to read that I wrote." (I didn't tell him it was a gospel tract.)

"I'd be happy to read it. Thank you."

When he saw what it was, he started to stutter and stammer, but it was too late to refuse it.

I met a famous basketball player and gave him one of my tracts, and he thanked me for it. Several weeks later he saw me at the service station, and he said, "I read your tract. Thank you."

You don't get to witness to a senator or a professional

basketball player until you witness to the woman behind the counter or the man at the dry cleaners.

Paul said, "But none of these things move me." Things that did not move Paul ought not to move us.

Every one of us is going to be tested and tried, and we'll be tempted to get the spiritual moving truck. But, by the help and grace of God, we need to remember what Paul said and not let tears or temptations cause us to get it. Testifying should keep us in God's will.

Don't get the moving truck yet!

14
It Takes Time to Finish the Job

"Watch thou in all things, endure afflictions, do the work of an evangelist, make full proof of thy ministry.

"For I am now ready to be offered, and the time of my departure is at hand.

"I have fought a good fight, I have finished my course, I have kept the faith:

"Henceforth there is laid up for me a crown of righteousness, which the Lord, the righteous judge, shall give me at that day: and not to me only, but unto all them also that love his appearing."—II Tim. 4:5–8.

There is a brief phrase in verse 7 which I would now like to consider: "I have finished my course."

Today in the work of God, it is extremely rare to locate a person who has remained at his post for an extended period of time. There are many that gather at the starting block, but only a small number get to or beyond the finishing line. To be a completed Christian, not just a started saint, is to be a minority in the family of God.

In II Timothy, chapter 4, we find the apostle Paul's solemn, final charge. I never come to this section of Scripture without being mindful that I am reading what I call "the swan song of a great servant of the Saviour."

In this chapter, Paul mentions four things that are coming:

> Christ is coming—vs. 1
> Apostasy is coming (and is here)—vss. 2–5
> Departure is coming—vss. 6–8
> Help is coming—vss. 9–22

As part of his description of his coming departure, Paul writes our heart-captivating, five-word text: "I have finished my course."

The sister verse of II Timothy 4:7 is Acts 20:24: "But none of these things move me, neither count I my life dear unto myself, so that I might finish my course with joy, and the ministry, which I have received of the Lord Jesus, to testify the gospel of the grace of God." That expresses Paul's desire articulated in words, while our text shows Paul's desire achieved in works.

D. L. Moody, that great and powerful preacher of yesteryear, once wrote these words in the margin of his Bible beside II Timothy 4:7: "A child cried because the eggs were all broken when the chickens were hatched, but they had accomplished their work."

One of the reasons that the apostle Paul is still remembered today is that he completed his course. But many preachers, Sunday school teachers and church bus drivers are soon forgotten because their course was not completed. Every Christian should strive to be like Brother Paul and finish their spiritual task.

There are three elements that will help the believer in his every effort to finish his course for God. I call them "factors for finishing."

Factor 1: Watching

"Watch thou in all things, endure afflictions, do the work of an evangelist, make full proof of thy ministry."—II Tim. 4:5.

The apostle Paul tells us that Timothy was to work on having his spiritual and physical eyes wide open, and he was to observe everything which took place around him.

The word "watch" is the Greek word *nepho*, and it is the same word used in I Peter 4:7. It is used in connection with the imminent return of the Lord Jesus Christ. It means "to be sober or to be vigilant"; thus, the tremendous truth communicated there is that the Christian is to keep his eyes peeled on the circumstances around him and the clouds above him.

Fanny J. Crosby, that great hymn writer, must have had the same reality upon her heart when she picked up the songwriter's pen and put on the songwriter's paper these heart-penetrating words:

> When Jesus comes to reward His servants,
>   Whether it be noon or night,
> Faithful to Him will He find us watching
>   With our lamps all trimmed and bright?
>
> O, can we say we are ready, brother,
>   Ready for the soul's bright Home?

169

Say, will He find you and me still watching,
Waiting, waiting when the Lord shall come?

The Bible says, "The end of all things is at hand: be ye therefore sober, and watch unto prayer" (I Pet. 4:7). It is scripturally impossible for the believer, while he is looking for the Lord to come, to leave off preaching, praying and presenting the Gospel to perishing souls.

If we are going to be *finishers* and not just *starters,* then we are going to have to plug into our lives this matter and this truth and this business of watching.

Awhile back I read a story about a Japanese dog that accompanied his master to the railroad station every morning, and then every evening he was back waiting for his master. One night the man died in another city. The dog, unable to comprehend that his master would not return, continued to go to the railroad station every evening and faithfully and patiently wait for his master's return. After an hour, he would sadly trot back home. He did this every evening for ten years.

The dog's faithfulness so impressed the Japanese people that the government erected a statue of the dog on the spot where he had waited for his master. Then they sent smaller statues to all the schools to remind them of the dog's faithfulness.

If a canine could for a decade watch for his master's return, surely we can watch for our Master's return as well!

Factor 2: Weathering

"But watch thou in all things, endure [weather] afflictions, do the work of an evangelist, make full proof of thy ministry."—II Tim. 4:5.

An element that will help every believer in his every effort for God is *weathering*. The apostle Paul tells us that Timothy was to have a determined, spiritual demeanor for his spiritual duty.

"Endure afflictions" makes it very plain to the serious servant of God that his service will not be a stroll through the park.

What Paul was telling Timothy was that he needed to be made of the right stuff, and God is telling us by way of His Word the same thing.

The Cork and the Whale
A little brown cork fell in the path of a whale
Who lashed it down with his angry tail.
But in spite of its blows, the cork quickly arose
And floated calmly before his nose.

Said the cork to the whale, "You may flap, you may frown,
But you'll never, never keep me down;
For I'm made of the stuff that is buoyant enough
To keep on floating instead of drown."

Friend, if we are going to give our every effort for God, we are going to have to determine that we are in this thing for the long haul and, come what may, we are going to weather the things that take place.

We've got a lot of starters, but what about the finishers? Many people start this, that and the other, but what about those that stick with it and finish? Many are in one ministry for one month, then go on to

171

another ministry for another month and yet another ministry the next month. Jumping from one ministry to another is not in God's plan. He wants us to understand what He wants us to do and then stick with it and stick at it!

A stem is a success because it sticks to one thing—the root. And, friend, if we are going to complete our every effort for God, then we're going to have to "endure afflictions."

There are several paramount things that God wants His children to deal with properly.

1. Providence. "Can thine heart endure, or can thine hands be strong, in the days that I shall deal with thee? I the LORD have spoken it, and will do it" (Ezek. 22:14).

The Heavenly Father wants to know how His children will do when He takes them by the hand and leads them from the high mountain into the low valley.

Let me say this about a valley: it is just a mountain turned upside down. It is a geographical fact that you cannot have a valley unless you have two mountains, one on either side.

A young man in London surrendered his life to Christ. He wanted to be used fully by the Lord, so he began preparing for the ministry. Before his ordination, he was required to preach a trial sermon to a select group of clergymen. The tenseness of the situation made him nervous, especially when he saw his beautiful fiancée in the audience.

In his anxiety, he lost his train of thought and failed to be approved. His rejection by the examining board was a stunning disappointment, and his grief increased when the young lady broke their engagement because he had done so poorly.

He fought a terrible battle with depression. After pouring out his complaint before God, he felt the burden lifted as he realized that the Lord was working out a blessed plan for his life.

He took the test again, and this time he was ordained into the ministry. Later, the profound preaching of G. Campbell Morgan moved the masses by its biblical depth and heartwarming appeal. He authored a good number of Bible commentaries and left a legacy of sermons that still stir the hearts of people.

There would be a good number of books missing from the fundamental preacher's study if Mr. Morgan had not learned that most essential lesson for a Christian: "endure afflictions."

What are you going to do when you are brought to those lowlands, those low times, those low spots in your Christian life? I read a church marquee that said, "If God brought me *to* it, God can bring me *through* it!"

How are you going to handle providence?

2. Paddling. "If ye endure chastening, God dealeth with you as with sons" (Heb. 12:7).

Both the blessings and the blisterings hold great lessons for the believer. If you only learn a lesson when God blesses you, then you are learning *half* of what you could learn in your Christian life. God uses blessings to teach us, but He also uses blisterings to teach us.

I got saved in a church that gave you the right hand

of fellowship and placed tithing envelopes in your left hand at the same time. As soon as I got up from the altar, I was given a box of tithing envelopes with the words: "Now, you fill these up, and we'll give you another box." I was only moments old in the Lord, and I was already being given tithing envelopes.

I thought, *I'll just work my way into this tithing thing; I'll start at one percent and work up to ten percent.* But the week I got saved, my car broke down. I took it for repairs, and the bill was the exact amount of what my tithe should have been! I learned that God gets His tithe whether I give it or whether He takes it.

By the way, don't try working your way up to ten percent; it doesn't work. The best thing is just to give the full amount from the beginning. Unfortunately, some Christians need to get their tithe repaired by the water heater man; some need to go to the hospital to get their tithe replaced by the surgeon.

If you don't get it, back to the woodshed you go. There are those who must be taken many times to the woodshed over things that should have been taken care of with only one trip, but God has to keep dealing with them. Whenever you go to the woodshed, there is apt to be bloodshed, so wouldn't it be easier to learn the lesson the first time?

3. Persecution. "Thou therefore endure hardness, as a good soldier of Jesus Christ" (II Tim. 2:3).

Anyone can serve God when people are tossing roses, but what about when those same people are throwing rotten eggs? Your biggest fan can become your biggest foe in twenty-four short hours.

One night after I had preached, a fellow came up to me and said, "Dr. Hamblin, would you sign my Bible?" I have probably signed thousands of Bibles, and I opened his to the flyleaf and pulled out a pen; but before I could begin, he said, "Wait a minute! Don't use your pen. I want you to use my pencil." That sounded kind of odd, but I signed his Bible in pencil and added God's personal phone number at the end: Jeremiah 33:3. When I handed him back his Bible and his pencil, he looked at me and said, "I have heard you preach enough times to know that I may have loved it tonight, but tomorrow night you may tick me off. If you do, I will erase your signature and your life verse from my Bible!" That's how he dealt with persecution. How do *you* deal with it?

In weathering afflictions, the things you will have to deal with are providence, paddlings and persecution.

Factor 3: Working

"But watch thou in all things, endure afflictions, do the work of an evangelist, make full proof of thy ministry."—
II Tim. 4:5.

The apostle Paul tells Timothy that he was to spend his spiritual sweat in seeing lost souls saved.

The Greek word for "evangelist" is *euaggelistes*, meaning "a preacher of the Gospel." Doing the work of an evangelist is the primary purpose of *every* preacher that steps into the pulpit to preach!

"And he [Jesus] said unto them, Go ye into all the world, and preach the gospel to every creature" (Mark 16:15). Friend, we need to understand that a factor for finishing is working.

I heard a preacher say, "A Christian is to be a 'creature-reacher.'" A Christian should never come to the wrong conclusion that the "work of an evangelist" is reserved for only someone with a calendar full of preaching dates, a wrinkled suit from traveling and dark circles under his eyes from exhaustion. The "work of an evangelist" reaches all the way from the Sunday school teacher to the ushers, choir members, musicians, church members and housekeeping staff. Every Christian is to do the "work of an evangelist."

It is sad when we don't have a burden for the lost, when our soul-winning fuel does not burn, when our soul-winning effort does not catch fire and increase. Soul winning is not as exciting as the temporal things in our lives, but it is eternal, and it should be the most exciting thing a Christian ever undertakes, because it is keeping people out of Hell!

Not long ago I was preaching on the last day of a Sword of the Lord conference. At the back of the large auditorium sat a child about five years old. I looked at this child, and he was locked into what I was saying; every time I looked at him, he was staring right back at me. I thought, *He's paying better attention than a lot of adults!* When the invitation was given, he pulled on his mother's skirt and said something to her. She answered him, but it seemed like he would not be denied, and they kept talking back and forth. I could see that something was happening in his soul.

The next afternoon I was at the airport waiting for my flight when my cell phone rang. It was that young boy: "We've got a little bit of a problem," he said.

I said, "What would that be?"

He said, "I believe God is calling me to preach. What should I do about it?"

I said, "Surrender, and let's pray about it now."

I bowed my head right there in the airport, and he bowed his head in his house, and we both got to the throne of grace at the same time. He raised the white flag of his will and surrendered to preach. Then he called his grandparents and told them that he'd been called to preach.

Now, this little fellow had written his own gospel tract. It had a cross on it and these words: "God loves you." He asked his mother to take him to the library, whereupon he walked up and down the aisles until he found a child older than himself.

He said, "Can you read?"

The boy said, "Yeah, I can read."

"Well, take this and read it, 'cause I wrote it."

That young man was Kyle Halleck, Dr. and Mrs. Wayne Halleck's grandson. I call him the future Lee Roberson.

If a five-year-old knows that he ought to do his best to keep people out of Hell, shouldn't we also be doing something about it?

A factor for finishing is working at getting people saved.

Four years after the *Titanic* went down, a young Scotsman rose in a meeting and said, "I am a survivor of the *Titanic*," and he told this story:

One of the passengers on the *Titanic* was Reverend John Harper, a preacher traveling to America to take the pastorate of the famed Moody Memorial Church. The year before, he had preached what was to have been a week-long meeting at the church, but they had had such a great meeting that it lasted for three months! When the church was in need of a pastor, they extended the call to John Harper, and he was making the voyage to America with his daughter and his sister-in-law. His wife had died the year before.

As the *Titanic* was sinking, John Harper ran up and down the decks of the ship, crying, "Women, children and the unsaved to the lifeboats!" He came across me and asked if I was saved. When I said no, he took off his life-jacket and put it on me, saying, "You need this more than I do!" and then gave me the Gospel.

I drifted alone on a spar that awful night when the tide brought alongside me another piece of wreckage. On it was John Harper.

Mr. Harper said, "Are you saved yet?"

I said, "No."

He said, "Believe on the Lord Jesus Christ, and thou shalt be saved!"

Then the wind and the waves carried him away. In a while the wind and the waves carried him back alongside me, and in a weakened voice, he asked again, "Are you saved?"

Again, I said, "No."

Once again Mr. Harper said, "Believe on the Lord Jesus Christ, and thou shalt be saved."

Again, the wind and waves carried John Harper away, and that was the last time anyone ever heard from him. But that night under a million stars, seemingly on dress parade, and with three miles of ocean beneath me, I believed on John Harper's Christ and was saved!"

John Harper used the factor of *working* to finish his course.

The apostle Paul was soon to say good-bye to this

world and hello to a heavenly world, but before he died, he said by the pen of inspiration and preservation, "I have finished my course."

Friend, don't you want to get to that place? Remember: our course—yours and mine—could end tonight.

I knew a young missionary on deputation. He was raising money to go to Cambodia, but his course suddenly ended. You don't know but that any day of this year could have its date inscribed upon your headstone.

We all want to get to verse 7: "I have fought a good fight, I have finished my course, I have kept the faith," but we don't get there unless we go through verse 5. That is the verse where we find the factors for finishing:

> *"Watch thou in all things, endure afflictions, do the work of an evangelist, make full proof of thy ministry."*

We can finish our course if we are watching, weathering and working.

15
There's a Time of Rewards

"And I saw heaven opened, and behold a white horse; and he that sat upon him was called Faithful and True, and in righteousness he doth judge and make war.

"His eyes were as a flame of fire, and on his head were many crowns; and he had a name written, that no man knew, but he himself.

"And he was clothed with a vesture dipped in blood: and his name is called The Word of God.

"And the armies which were in heaven followed him upon white horses, clothed in fine linen, white and clean.

"And out of his mouth goeth a sharp sword, that with it he should smite the nations: and he shall rule them with a rod of iron: and he treadeth the winepress of the fierceness and wrath of Almighty God.

"And he hath on his vesture and on his thigh a name written, KING OF KINGS, AND LORD OF LORDS."—Rev. 19:11–16.

If there is an event that will stand above all the rest in Heaven, it would have to be the experience when the saint gives back to the Saviour his special garland. The same brow that had a crown of thorns placed upon it on earth will have a crown of triumph placed upon it in eternity.

The child of God's greatest motivation for service should be to obtain the garland that he can secure and then give back to the Son of God.

The word translated "crowns" is plural and is where we get our word *diadem*. Monarchs who claimed authority over more than one country wore more than one crown. It was Ptolemy Philometor who, when he entered Antioch as a conqueror, wore a triple crown: two for Egypt and one for Asia.

An individual will only feel the full import of the phrase "and on his head were many crowns," when he considers that this will take place *after* crowns have been presented to worthy believers at the judgment seat of Christ.

Second Corinthians 5:10 says, "For we must all appear before the judgment seat of Christ; that every one may receive the things done in his body, according to that he hath done, whether it be good or bad."

Those of us who are saved will be able to place our crown upon the head of the Lord Jesus Christ. What could be more rewarding than that?

In the New Testament we find five crowns listed:

The crown of life. *"Fear none of those things which thou shalt suffer: behold, the devil shall cast some of you into prison, that ye may be tried; and ye shall have tribulation ten days: be thou faithful unto death, and I will give thee a crown of life."*—Rev. 2:10.

The crown of glory. *"And when the chief Shepherd shall appear, ye shall receive a crown of glory that fadeth not away."*—I Pet. 5:4.

The crown of rejoicing. *"For what is our hope, or joy, or crown of rejoicing? Are not even ye in the presence of our Lord Jesus Christ at his coming?"*—I Thess. 2:19.

The crown of righteousness. *"Henceforth there is laid up for me a crown of righteousness, which the Lord, the righteous judge, shall give me at that day: and not to me only, but unto all them also that love his appearing."*—II Tim. 4:8.

The crown of moral integrity. *"And every man that striveth for the mastery is temperate in all things. Now they do it to obtain a corruptible crown; but we an incorruptible."*—I Cor. 9:25.

Let's look at these crowns and who will receive them so they can return them to Jesus.

I. The Tortured Martyr

"Fear none of those things which thou shalt suffer: behold, the devil shall cast some of you into prison, that ye may be tried; and ye shall have tribulation ten days: be thou faithful unto death, and I will give thee a crown of life."—Rev. 2:10.

The Lord Jesus Christ promised the believers in the church at Smyrna that if they lost their lives because of persecution, they would receive the "crown of life."

It is important for us to understand that Smyrna was the second of the local churches in Asia and represents the second period of the church age. Its name means "myrrh" or "bitterness." It was from the first to the fourth century that Smyrna suffered persecution under the Roman emperors.

It was in the city of Smyrna in A.D.168 that Polycarp, that great Christian firebrand, was put to death. Some think that he was the last living person to have carried on a personal conversation with John the Beloved.

Friend, you and I need to understand that the tortured martyr will place his crown upon the Lord Jesus Christ's head.

Second Timothy 2:3 says, "Thou therefore endure hardness, as a good soldier of Jesus Christ."

When believers look through the telescope of Scripture and see saints getting the garland of life, it should make them ashamed for giving up over a slight, a snub or a slander because of their fundamental stand.

The Christian of the twenty-first century who makes America his home doesn't have a clue of what suffering for Jesus is all about.

In the fall of 2002, I was in a revival meeting. On Friday night while I was preaching, an eight-year-old boy and his mother were seated on the third row of the right-hand side of the pulpit. The whole time I was preaching, that child was wiggling and squirming and disrupting the service. His mother tried everything she could to control him. Finally as she grabbed him, he hockey-checked his mother, and she slid all the way down the pew, nearly landing in the floor.

That was about all I could take. In a sweet, soft-spoken way, I stopped and said, "This young man in the service is not only distracting others, he's now disturbing me. I don't have anything worth listening to, but God has a whole lot to say that's worth listening to. Son, you need to straighten up and listen."

About that time his mother grabbed him and dragged him out of the church.

When the service was over, the pastor came to me and said, "There's a telephone call for you." I took it in his study. It was the mother of the child who had disturbed the service, and as soon as she heard my voice, she began to curse at me.

Now, I was on her side, I had tried to help her out, I was trying to be a blessing to her, but she didn't see it that way. I've never heard some of the words she used, and I've had a number of folks cuss me out over the years.

I finally was able to get a word in, and I said, "I would like to come to your house and talk to you in person."

She said, "I dare you to come," and she slammed down the phone.

I told the pastor that we needed to go talk to this lady. He said, "Oh, no we don't!"

I said, "Oh, yes we do!"

"Oh, no. You don't understand. That happens about once a month around here."

I convinced him to go with me. They lived out in the country, and as we drove up the gravel driveway, I saw on the porch this woman holding a long leash. On the other end of the leash was a pet goat. When I came around the van and walked onto the porch, that goat jumped right on top of me.

Now, she had the leash and could have pulled him back, but she didn't feel inspired to do so. While I was standing there with the goat on top of me (and he was trying to eat my lapel at the same time), she began to take cussing to a lower level, and she let me have it with both barrels. All the while this was happening on the porch, the kid that had caused so much trouble was looking out through the window with a devilish grin on his face.

She said, "My son said I'm supposed to let you have it!"

I said, "Ten years from now, your son will probably tell you to let the warden have it too!"

Even so, this was not what the Christian martyrs went through. If you want to know what true persecution is, read *Foxe's Book of Martyrs;* the first dozen or so pages will show you that Christians today haven't a clue of what it means to suffer for Jesus.

I found a small paragraph in that book about John Stillman. It reads:

> John Stillman charged for speaking against the worshipping, praying and offering of sacrifices to images and denying the carnal and corporal presence in the sacrament of Christ's memorial. He called John Wycliffe, another outstanding reformer, a saint in Heaven. [In John Stillman's day, as in our own, there was a religious monstrosity that thought they had the power to make people saints. No one is made a saint by a church; you are a saint by Christ!] Delivered unto the sheriff of London to be openly burned. 1518.

When people were martyred in those days, they were not tied to a pole, but chained to it, because ropes would have burned through when the fire was lit. Sometimes a bag of gunpowder was placed over the head of the martyr, and the extreme heat or a stray spark from the fire would ignite the gunpowder and literally blow off his head.

John Stillman will in eternity receive a crown that will outshine a billion suns.

II. The True Minister

"And when the chief Shepherd shall appear, ye shall receive a crown of glory that fadeth not away."—I Pet. 5:4.

The Lord Jesus Christ promised the preacher that if he remained precise in his ministry, he would receive a "crown of glory." This tremendous truth should make the heart of every pastor, evangelist or missionary glad that God does not miss the spiritual, emotional and physical energy that he expends in the work of God.

Some people think that being in the ministry is easy. Now, there isn't any job *better* than preaching, but it takes a lot of spiritual, emotional and physical energy.

There are times when right before I'm introduced to preach, I begin to think, *Physically, I don't have it! I am worn-out and sapped!* But God in His wisdom and grace gives me that window of strength and power and wherewithal to help me with what I've got to do.

Last year I preached 377 times, taking off one week for our annual family vacation, and I am glad that God is aware of what I need and what I give out in serving Him.

If he will stay true and faithful and loyal, there is a crown awaiting the true minister, and he will place the crown of glory upon the brow of his Saviour.

Not everyone who calls himself a preacher *is* a preacher. Let me give you three things that mark a genuine man of God.

187

1. He's fundamental. "Preach the word; be instant in season, out of season; reprove, rebuke, exhort with all longsuffering and doctrine" (II Tim. 4:2). A bona fide preacher gives his doctrinal statement every time he puts an open Bible upon the pulpit and preaches from it.

When preachers came to hear me preach in my early ministry, they'd ask for a doctrinal statement. I would take them to my tape table and randomly pick out a tape and say, "Here it is." I thought that every time I preached I was giving a doctrinal statement.

2. He is firm. "Them that sin rebuke before all, that others also may fear" (I Tim. 5:20). Phony clergymen never cry out against the sinful practices of the world and the church, but a genuine man of God always is firm and takes his stand with the Scriptures.

There might be times when your preacher preaches something that hits you right between the eyes. That is not the time for you to go looking for another church or to move your membership or to begin looking for another pastor. If your preacher calls sin by its name and tells it straight from the Bible, that's the time to follow the leadership of the Holy Spirit and hit the old-time altar and do business with God.

3. He is fiery. "But watch thou in all things, endure afflictions, do the work of an evangelist, make full proof of thy ministry" (II Tim. 4:5). An honest preacher always has a furnace in his heart when it comes to preaching; and I believe honest, fiery preaching is the answer for the Christian, for the church and for our country.

Preachers and their style of preaching are as different as fingerprints.

One preacher introduced me like this: "You don't hear Dr. Hamblin preach; you experience him." A lady said one time after I was done preaching, "I went home last night after the service and watched a boxing match, and I believe one of the boxer's has stolen all your moves." Another lady said to me, "Dr. Hamblin, you move around so much when you preach that I get seasick."

But the genuine marks of a man of God are that he is fundamental, firm and fiery.

Dr. J. Wilbur Chapman used to tell of the preacher who often spoke on the subject of sin, mincing no words, but calling it "the abominable thing that God hates." One from his congregation came to him and urged him to stop using that ugly word. "We wish you would not speak so plainly about sin. Our young people hearing you will be more likely to indulge in it. Call it something else, such as inhibition, error or mistake."

The preacher would go to the medicine cupboard and produce a small bottle of strychnine which had on it a red label marked "poison" and ask, "Would you suggest that I change the label and put one on it that reads 'wintergreen'?"

Preachers who turn their guns on sin in any form, on transgression in any dwelling place, on iniquity in the heart, will in eternity receive the accolades of a pearly city.

III. The Tearful Messenger

"For what is our hope, or joy, or crown of rejoicing? Are not even ye in the presence of our Lord Jesus Christ at his coming?"—I Thess. 2:19.

Another person who will place his special garland upon the Son of God's head is the tearful messenger.

The apostle Paul tells us that the Lord Jesus Christ promised him a "crown of rejoicing" because he had personally brought Thessalonian believers to the cross. Brother Paul's children in the faith were his pleasure on earth and will be his prize in eternity.

Herein lies the secret of the Christian life. Those you reach for Christ will bring you hope and joy here and will carry you to a crown of rejoicing over there. I'm glad that we can have joy in serving Jesus.

Why is it that so many Christians seemingly have no hope and no joy? I don't want to ask them how they are, because they'll tell me; and when they're done with their explanation of all their problems, I'm ready to say "ouch" and go on vacation.

Some say, "Well, I have joy, but I don't believe in expressing it. I don't think we ought to get revved up about heavenly things. We ought to be dignified Christians."

Your face is a good barometer of the atmosphere of your heart. If your heart is happy, your face will radiate happiness. If your heart is right, your face will be right.

Dr. John R. Rice said, "The long-faced Christian with no joy is a mighty poor signboard for Christ."

Those you reach for Christ will cause you open joy here and will bring you to a crown of rejoicing over there.

When you win people to the Lord, you automatically have hope and joy. And it is the tearful messenger who will place his crown upon the Lord Jesus Christ's head.

Psalm 126:6 says, "He that goeth forth and weepeth, bearing precious seed, shall doubtless come again with rejoicing, bringing his sheaves with him."

In the fall of 1982, I was asked to hold a protracted revival meeting. I'd been in evangelism one year, and I had no idea what a protracted meeting was, but I agreed to do it. A protracted meeting is one that has a definite starting time but no definite stopping time. God was in my ignorance, because if I'd known what it was, I wouldn't have gone. I preached Sunday morning, Sunday night and all through the week for three straight weeks!

At that point in time, I only had seven sermons, so when I'd preached those seven, I rearranged the material and retitled them and reapproached them.

One afternoon the host preacher and I went to call on a man who was a new convert but who hadn't yet followed the Lord in believer's baptism. The young man invited us into his home and introduced us to a visiting friend, but the friend never even acknowledged us; he just kept reading his newspaper.

We sat in the living room, and the preacher began to deal with the believer about being baptized. The man said he would come that night and be baptized.

Then the pastor began to speak to the man's unsaved friend. He just kept reading his paper and ignoring the pastor. After a while, the pastor nodded at me; I took that to mean that it was my turn. I waded right in and began to witness to him, but I got the same response.

I was getting nowhere fast. I stopped, and the other preacher started in again. I thought to myself, *We're wasting our time. Here is a man who is totally ignoring us.* Just as I had that thought, the preacher hit the floor and crawled on his hands and knees to that man. He threw his arms around that man's legs and witnessed to him again, weeping unashamedly.

The newspaper was lowered, and we saw that the unbeliever was also weeping. He hit the floor beside that preacher and was gloriously converted.

"And on his head were many crowns." Where did all those crowns come from? They came from believers who got them at the judgment seat and gave them back to the Son of God.

I've preached all this to make this one statement: The number of crowns that He wears that day will be the number of crowns that we earn and give back to Him at the judgment seat of Christ.

Will He have one less crown because you or I were not faithful in our service to Him?

16
When Time Shall Be No More

"And I saw a new heaven and a new earth: for the first heaven and the first earth were passed away; and there was no more sea.

"And I John saw the holy city, new Jerusalem, coming down from God out of heaven, prepared as a bride adorned for her husband.

"And I heard a great voice out of heaven saying, Behold, the tabernacle of God is with men, and he will dwell with them, and they shall be his people, and God himself shall be with them, and be their God.

"And God shall wipe away all tears from their eyes; and there shall be no more death, neither sorrow, nor crying, neither shall there be any more pain: for the former things are passed away.

"And he that sat upon the throne said, Behold, I make all things new. And he said unto me, Write: for these words are true and faithful.

"And he said unto me, It is done. I am Alpha and Omega, the beginning and the end. I will give unto him that is athirst of the fountain of the water of life freely.

"He that overcometh shall inherit all things; and I will be his God, and he shall be my son.

193

> *"But the fearful, and unbelieving, and the abominable, and murderers, and whoremongers, and sorcerers, and idolaters, and all liars, shall have their part in the lake which burneth with fire and brimstone: which is the second death."—Rev. 21:1-8.*

Heaven is a place of exquisite beauty. In picture-like words the Holy Spirit paints the gates of pearl, foundations of gems and the street of gold upon the canvas of the Scriptures. This City's splendor is magnified by the troublesome things that *cannot* be found within its limits.

The apostle John is the inspired writer of the Book of Revelation, the last book of the Bible. Because of his testimony for the Lord Jesus Christ, he was exiled to the rocky island of Patmos. While on this isle, he experienced the unique privilege of witnessing many future events.

> *"I John, who also am your brother, and companion in tribulation, and in the kingdom and patience of Jesus Christ, was in the isle that is called Patmos, for the word of God, and for the testimony of Jesus Christ.*
>
> *"I was in the Spirit on the Lord's day, and heard behind me a great voice, as of a trumpet."—Rev. 1:9, 10.*

In the Greek language, the word "Revelation" (vs. 1:1) means "to remove the veil." John not only removes the veil from prophetic events, but also from the pearly City. The same Bible that tells us what *is* in Heaven also tells us what is *not* in Heaven, and under the direct inspiration of the Holy Spirit, in the last two chapters of Revelation, John writes seven (God's number of perfection) things that will be missing from the New Jerusalem:

"No more sea"—21:1
"No more death"—vs. 4
"No more...sorrow"—vs. 4
"No more...crying"—vs. 4
"No more...pain"—vs. 4
"No [more] night"—vs. 25
"No more curse"—22:3

I am thankful for what *is* in Heaven and for the things that will be *missing* from the New Jerusalem.

There are three 'no mores' of Heaven that will encourage the heart of the child of God. All of us can use a good dose of encouragement. Dr. Malone always said, "When a Christian tells me that he never gets discouraged, I think to myself, *Yes, and you lie as well!*" There are times when Christians are blue and down and feel bad, but, oh, there are some things that cannot be found in Heaven, and that ought to encourage our hearts.

The three 'no mores' of Heaven are found in Revelation 21:4.

I. No More Separation

"God shall wipe away all tears from their eyes; and there shall be no more death."

There is no separation in Heaven. Since the dawn of time, death has been the feared enemy of mankind. It has divided his family and his friends. The grave is no respecter of persons. The names of the young and old, the rich and poor, can all be found in the obituary section of today's world newspapers.

"Wherefore, as by one man sin entered into the

195

world, and death by sin; and so death passed upon all men, for that all have sinned." (Rom. 5:12). When Adam disobeyed God by eating from the Tree of the Knowledge of Good and Evil in the Garden of Eden, he brought the sentence of death upon his offspring.

That one sin brought about the moral ruin of the race. And because of Adam's sin, we are closer to the grave today than we were yesterday. If Jesus stays His coming and God is good to us and gives us another day, we will be closer to the grave tomorrow than we are today.

Since that first sin, the death angel has been beating out the death march for mankind. We die because of the sin of Adam.

When we look around, we see the harsh repercussions of Adam's rebellion. The bodies of our loved ones are in funeral homes; the corpses of our acquaintances ride in hearses; the remains of our friends are in cemeteries. Barring the return of the Lord Jesus Christ, death will invade every home; but none of those heartwrenching things will ever take place in Heaven, because there shall be "no more death."

If there is an unemployment line in Heaven, then funeral directors, hearse drivers and gravediggers must be standing in it.

Dr. R. G. Lee, a great and powerful man of God, had the ability to paint pictures with his words. He once told the sad story about how death had invaded the home of a young couple.

He said, "Years ago I led to Christ a lovely young woman and man. I baptized them that same night.

Later, I married them. A year later a little child came into their home, whose little hands had a mighty grip on their hearts. One night, around midnight, the father phoned me from the hospital and said that the seven-month-old child was critically ill. With agony in his voice, the young father said, 'Pastor, we need you so. Please come to the hospital, room 520.'

"I went to the hospital and found two concerned doctors there; they seemed helpless and hopeless to rescue the child from death. With all eyes fastened upon the little face and with skillful hands ministering, the little one passed away.

"The undertakers came in and wrapped up the little body in a shawl and started out the door. The mother cried, 'Oh, let me have my baby just one more night. Please, just one more night!' The distressed husband turned to me and said, 'Preacher, what shall I tell her?' I said, 'Let her have him just one more night.' The undertaker put the child in the mother's arms.

"I went home with them. The mother sat with that little dead baby in her lap and cooed and talked to him, but there was no light of life in his eyes, no laughter in his body, no warmth in his frame. But she had her child for just one more night."

After hearing that story, I thought about how in Heaven no mother will ever again hold a dead baby, for in Heaven there is no death.

II. No More Sorrow

"There shall be no more...sorrow."

Sadness is an emotion that everyone feels. We can

197

identify with the psalmist when he said, "My tears have been my meat day and night" (Ps. 42:3). At one time or another we have sat at the meal of remorse. You don't have to take many steps to find someone with a burden, and ere the sun set this day, someone's heart will be broken. But, thank God, we are going to a place where no heart will ever break or be burdened! Won't it be wonderful one day to say farewell to sorrow and heartache; we'll say good-bye to burdened souls.

There are at least three things that bring sorrow to the Christian's soul.

1. Impatience toward deliverance. "How long shall I take counsel in my soul, having sorrow in my heart daily? how long shall mine enemy be exalted over me?" (Ps. 13:2). Needless grief comes when you expect God to work on your time schedule, but His watch is not set to yours. Our watch is to be set to His time! As I said in the first chapter, God is never early, and He is never late; He is always right on time.

2. Unsaved family members. "I have great heaviness and continual sorrow in my heart. For I could wish that myself were accursed from Christ for my brethren, my kinsmen according to the flesh" (Rom. 9:2, 3).

No burden weighs as heavily as the burden for lost loved ones. That's the kind of sorrow we need a wagonload of for all the lost, especially family members.

3. Longing for wealth. "The love of money is the root of all evil: which while some coveted after, they have erred from the faith, and pierced themselves

198

through with many sorrows" (I Tim. 6:10). It's not the money that is evil; it's the *love* of money that is evil. The person who lives for riches will die with remorse. How many fine cars can one person drive? How many big homes can you live in? How many fine suits of clothes can you wear?

The most important things in this preacher's life are the things that are spiritual, not material.

If you got out of bed this morning, God was good to you. If you had a bite to eat, God has been good to you. If you are reading this book, He has been good to you. Nothing—not cars, homes or clothing—can take the place of any of these things. Our biggest blessings are spiritual and not material.

Oh, how glad I am that I'm going to a land where I don't have to sorrow, where my heart will not break, where I will live eternally within the limits of the City where there are no broken hearts.

F. M. Lehman wrote:

> There's no disappointment in Heaven,
> No weariness, sorrow or pain,
> No hearts that are bleeding and broken,
> No song with a minor refrain.
> The clouds of our earthly horizon
> Will never appear in the sky,
> For all will be sunshine and gladness,
> With never a sob or a sigh.

Not long after I got saved, I was around a number of Christians with gray hair, and they talked about Heaven and the New Jerusalem and the Glory Land. I remember how tears would well up in their eyes and their voices would choke with emotion. Even though I knew I was going there, I wondered, *Why do they weep when they talk about Heaven?* Then God let my heart break, and I realized why they wept: there is a land beyond the stars where we never weep or cry, a land where we never again will experience sorrow.

The weeping we've done today or this past week is just for this life. There will be weeping until Jesus comes, but if you are saved, you are going to a place where you will never weep again!

There is a Chinese parable about a woman who lost her only son. She was grief-stricken out of all reason. She made her sorrow a wailing wall. Finally she went to a wise old philosopher who said to her, "I'll give you back your son if you'll bring me some mustard seeds. However, the seeds must come from a home where there has never been sorrow."

Eagerly she began her search, going from house to house, but in every case she learned that a loved one had been lost.

"How selfish I've been in my grief," she said.

Sorrow is common to all, but when the Christian arrives in Heaven, he will learn that there happiness and not heartache is common to all.

No more sorrow.

III. No More Sickness

"Neither shall there be any more pain: for the former things are passed away."

More people have suffered in this world because of illness than any other single thing. It is responsible for crippled limbs and fevered brows, for wheelchairs, crutches and pain. But the saved have been given a precious promise from their Heavenly Father that discomfort will last for only a short period of time.

The Bible says, "Our light affliction, which is but for a moment, worketh for us a far more exceeding and eternal weight of glory" (II Cor. 4:17). That's a promise from the Heavenly Father! That word "moment" means "a minute, fleeting portion of time."

When a child of God is diagnosed with an incurable disease, hallelujah; it's only for a moment. When a saint can no longer do what he once did, hallelujah; it's only for a moment. When a Christian lies on a hospital bed, hallelujah; it's only for a moment. What the child of God goes through in this life is but for a moment when you lay it alongside eternity.

Sick Christian, you will be well longer than you've been sick; you will be healthier longer than you've endured broken health.

A distinguished painter was conducting a class for aspiring artists. He was speaking on the subject of artistic composition. He emphasized that it was wrong to portray a woodland, a forest or a wilderness without painting into it a pathway out of the trees.

He said, "When a true artist draws any kind of picture, even a landscape, he always gives a way out; otherwise, the tangle of trees and the trackless spaces depress and dismay the onlooker."

My friend, God has painted a way out for the believer who is lying on a bed of affliction, and that way out is *up!* No more sickness.

The same Bible that tells me about the street of gold and gates of pearl and walls of jasper also tells me that in Heaven there is no death, there are no broken hearts and there are no crippled bodies. That ought to encourage the heart of every Christian. That ought to cause an unsaved person to realize that he should get saved.

In I Corinthians 15:1–4, we read what the Gospel is: the death, burial and resurrection of the Lord Jesus Christ. He died for you; He was buried, and He rose again from the dead that you might be saved. If you are lost, this is as *close* to Heaven as you are ever going to get—this is it! If you are not saved, why not get saved and go with God's children to a place where there are some things missing—sorrow, separation and sickness?

For a complete list of books available from the Sword of the Lord, write to Sword of the Lord Publishers, P. O. Box 1099, Murfreesboro, Tennessee 37133.

(800) 251-4100
(615) 893-6700
FAX (615) 848-6943
www.swordofthelord.com